Long Way to go for a Date

by

Henry Makow

SILAS GREEN

silas_green@go.com

Dedicated to my mother,

Helen (Ickcowicz) Makow

(1919-1983)

Published by Silas Green
silas_green@go.com

cover photo of Cecilia, used with permission.

Manufactured in Canada

Canadian Cataloguing in Publication Data
Makow, Henry, 1949–
    A long way to go for a date
    ISBN 0-9687725-0-1

1. Makow, Henry, 1949–
2. Intercountry marriage—Manitoba—Winnipeg.
3. Mail order brides—Manitoba—Winnipeg.
3. Mail order brides—Philippines.
I. Title.

HQ1032.M34 2000   306.84'5'09712743   c00-920195-5

Overture

Club Fantasy.

About a dozen young men are seated below a stage. The young stripper has completed her act and is stark naked. The love-starved men wave dollar and two-dollar coins and put them between their teeth. The girl crouches on her knees before each of them. Using her hands, she takes the coin in her breasts. For a fleeting moment, the man has a tantalizing brush with feminine tenderness and love. I was that man. The scene is a metaphor for love today.

Prologue

Feeling better due to the stock market rebound, I phone Cheryl, wife of my friend Todd.

I start by saying I appreciate her concern. She is anticipating my next line: mind your own business.

Instead, I agree to talk about my upcoming trip to the Philippines to meet my "pen pal" Cecilia, an 18-year-old girl. I am 48.

When we meet for coffee, I thank her for extending herself.

"Look," she says. "I've watched your relationships for years and pretty well could see what was wrong."

OK, what was wrong with my marriage?

"Lack of passion. It was kind of functional. She did her thing. You did yours."

I am surprised. She hit the nail on the head.

And Susan?

"The opposite. Too much passion. She took advantage of you."

Right again.

"And now you're going to yet another extreme. You're looking for someone subservient. You'll enjoy it for a while but you'll get sick of it. She won't be close to your intellectual match. You bore easily. You bore really fast."

I ponder this while she continues:

"It's a big insult for North American women to see our men going for Asian women. We are very upset. We were taught to take control of our lives, to have a 50/50 share of power. Finally we learn to play this game, brave it out and now men are choosing traditional partners."

I tell her that I corresponded with liberated women on the net. They have a mental image of what they can love and they try to make you fit into it. You have to be so tall and look a certain way. You have to be a hero: a novelist, a professional, a filmmaker, a CEO.

Well, I won't jump through hoops for love. I'll do what I want. There is something appealing about a woman who loves you simply because you look after her. She doesn't have to own you body and soul. Liberated women are too much. They're too demanding.

Cheryl agrees that the female preoccupation with success is sickening.

Every liberated woman is a Chinese puzzle, I say. Too complicated, too much history, too many complexes. Cecilia said, I am a simple woman. I want someone who will understand my shortcomings. I don't expect you to be perfect.

She called the other night from the Philippines to say she'd won a local beauty contest, "Miss Malalag, 1997." (I congratulated her, overcoming misgivings about the effect of being a beauty queen on her character.)

I was able to say to her, "I can't talk now. I'm with friends."

She accepted it! I was as pleased with my own bravado as with her deference. A feminist would have bawled me out: "I'm calling you from half-way-around-the-world and you can't talk! Do you know how long I waited to use this phone? You bastard!" (This is what I'm used to.)

"They're subservient because they're poor," Cheryl says.

No, they're brought up that way. They're like that with poor men they marry.

"But a relationship requires constant stimulation or it becomes boring," Cheryl warns.

I'm not looking for "stimulation" in a mate, I tell her. I read books for that. I want to love and be loved. Feminists are the ones who are looking for intellectual stimulation.

Cheryl asks why I didn't find a mate in Winnipeg.

There are many reasons.

1) My addiction to gambling in stock options distracted me.

2) I am attracted to women under 35 who think I am too old. Sexual attraction is an important element in a male-female relationship. Nature, for obvious reasons, has bestowed this appeal on women of childbearing age. I get older but the women I find attractive don't.

3) My failure to recognize that I needed a traditional woman, one that builds her life around a man. I had been   looking for my "equal."

4) The fact that I work at home and don't meet anyone.

5) The fact that the city is frozen six months of the year. Everyone hibernates.

I tried the *dateline* service in the newspaper.

My first ad was headed "*Lots to Give Right Woman*". I wanted a woman age 25-45 who was graceful, intelligent, attractive and had a sense of humor. I described myself and promised revelry, love and travel.

This yielded a couple of messages from 40-something women whose gravelly voices were a turn-off. One woman who sounded feminine on the phone had shoulders wider than mine.

I tried a different tack to lure the younger set. The second ad was headed "*Ready for Babies.*" This also failed miserably. Apparently I am too old for North American women. I am no longer a player.

I turned to cyberspace and posted a profile on Jewish Singles on AOL. I used my hunkiest picture, taken 10 years ago.

A woman reading my profile could deduce that I was attractive, intelligent, rich, funny, loving and idealistic. I said I wanted a woman under 35 because I hadn't given up on children.

There were two responses from women in their early thirties. One referred me to her web site, which had received 2000 "hits." This degree of cyber promiscuity was off-putting.

The second "younger" woman was a PBS producer in New York. I ran afoul of her by disparaging the profession of psychology. (This is another reason I think women should postpone university until after they marry and have children.)

* * *

There are probably deeper reasons why I had to go 8500 miles to find love.

I know there is something pathetic about a middle-aged man who complains he felt "unloved" since childhood. But there is a direct line between that feeling and my actions.

Leonard Cohen wrote somewhere that, "It starts with your family and then it comes down to your soul." My father and mother were Polish Jews whose lives were uprooted by the holocaust. They met after the war in Switzerland, and like many holocaust survivors married too soon.

They immigrated to Canada in 1950 and focused on building a new life. The atmosphere at home was geared to hard work and achievement. There was little of the leisure or joy of families who have been in America for generations.

When I was a baby, my dad wouldn't let my mother feed me when I was hungry. All the books said children should be disciplined to eat at set times. I would cry out my lungs and then be too exhausted to eat at the proper hour. Is it any wonder I felt unloved? Then, my mother had a business importing watchstraps. While she was out selling, I was left at the homes of babysitters who also left me to cry.

As a child I deliberately caused trouble in order to get love. I had a gang called the "bubble gang" – rhyming with trouble – dedicated to mischief. Once my father chased me for blocks with a stick. He dragged me home for a beating. But instead of spanking me, he broke down and wept. That's the kind of child I was.

At age 10, the police came calling. We were living in Switzerland where my father had returned for his Ph.D. I had been breaking into boarding schools with a friend; and, pushing logs off the mountainside, smashing fences below. Our fathers had to fish the logs out of the ravine and transport them back to the hilltop.

Returning to Canada, I realized trouble making was not the best way. I decided to make a fresh start. I would become a model child. Within six months I was an "A" student. I began writing a weekly syndicated newspaper column for 38 newspapers called "Ask Henry."

It was an advice-to-parents column on how to raise children.

I was 11 years old. I had learned a false lesson: you get love through achievement. I didn't have other families to compare with. Outwardly everything seemed normal. But where there is an absence of love, there is an absence of intimacy. We walked around in psychic suits of armor.

* * *

My teen and twenties coincided with the 1960's and 70's. I was extremely idealistic. Like many youths, I was on a mission to discover the meaning of life and save the world.

Enrolled in a Ph.D. program at the University of Toronto, I spent my time having mystical visions on marijuana and reading. I seriously considered becoming a monk.

Although I had lived with a woman for a year when I was 19, I had little other experience until I married at age 32. I idealized women and saw love in religious terms. I was too serious and missed many opportunities to have fulfilling sexual relationships.

Feminism confused me and retarded my personal development. It made me look for an "equal", a *counterpart* (a female me) instead of a *complement* (someone very different, and feminine). Because of this, I was looking for *myself* in a relationship. Thus I put women I liked on a pedestal and gave up my power to them. I didn't understand masculinity. I didn't know how to relate to women.

I will always remember one afternoon at the Robarts Library Reading Room when I saw a beautiful young woman sitting at a desk. She melted in my gaze. She was ripe for the taking. But, approaching a woman on the basis of sexual attraction was foreign to me. It was frowned upon. No wonder I remained unloved!

No wonder I fell for Cecilia. I had to make up for 12 years I spent with my head in the clouds.

To grow emotionally, *we need to be loved.* Emotionally, I remained a case of retarded development.

CHAPTER 1

Not Every Man
Can Live Out
his Fantasies

Winnipeg, Dec.4, 1997.

My sister Anya, 44, drives me to the airport.

"Not every man can live out his fantasies," she says.

She implies that I will discover they are impractical, ridiculous, and illusory. Then, hopefully, I will settle down and act my age.

In the waiting area, two guys with snowboards flirt with an attractive blonde who is gobbling a bag of Doritos like a missed meal.

"Hey, Doritos! My favorite food!" one says.

She gives him a tolerant smile as our boarding call is announced.

She is the most attractive woman on the plane, and I am seated next to her, one seat between us. She is about 32, cute, a cheerleader type, her face getting a little puffy. She is sporting a big diamond ring. The three seats are like a magnet and I definitely feel the positive-negative sexual attraction.

She is lost in her *En Route* magazine and I have nothing to say to her.

As the plane lifts off for Vancouver, I reflect on my day. Market down again. My confidence must not be based on money. I am going on a journey. I am naked. I am carrying everything I have. I am smart, capable, confident, strong!

I had picked up my son Josh at school. Eleven and short for his age, he has a crush on a girl in his class. "When I talk to her, I feel like standing on my tiptoes," he says.

After supper, he goes home to his mother. My eyes follow him as he walks away in the snow. Four weeks till I see you again, son.

I printed letters to eight other Filipino women. They are my "Plan B" in case Cecilia doesn't work out. Ruth is 24 and has a child. She describes herself as unfortunate in love. She says she is "creative, smart and thrifty" as if to say the child won't be a burden.

Millie, 22, lives in Manila. She writes, "I don't care about my man's age, just his soul." That impresses me.

The flight to Vancouver takes 3 hours. Across the aisle, a man with a laptop scrolls over his company's financial targets for 1998 neatly divided into 10 categories and 10 stages.

A beer gives me the courage to talk to the blonde. Linda turns out to be quite nice. She teaches high school outside Winnipeg. Married to an accountant, she has no children. "I couldn't handle kids day and night," she says.

She seems like the typical modern woman. She says her goal is self-fulfillment.

This is achieved by: 1) Relationships which include her marriage, but also friends and family. 2) Her career. 3) Children.

"Women are not brought up to serve husband and kids any more," she says.

She and her husband make decisions together. They each have their own cars. He's a Ford man. She likes Toyota Four-Wheelers. They have a custom built house in the country.

The more she talks, the more she seems to be describing a merger.

Its purpose: a better lifestyle. Her marriage is about security and comfort. Does she love her husband? It hardly seems relevant.

She is going to Vancouver to visit a friend. "If I didn't have an equal relationship, I wouldn't be traveling alone," she says pathetically.

I reveal the purpose of my trip. My problem is younger women think 48 is 68. She confirms this. She says Filipino women don't have the option to be independent. Men like me are a way to better their lives.

In other words, I am being used because Cecilia has no other options. And I'm also using her. It's helpful to get a modern woman's perspective.

I compare Linda's ideas about fulfillment with my mother, a traditional woman.

Mom used to say she found fulfillment by loving (and serving) in order of priority: 1) my father; 2) her children; 3) Canada; 4) Israel.

She left herself off her own list. She was *too* selfless. She asked for nothing so we took her for granted. She should have been third on her own list and made some demands. She didn't teach us to respect her. For example, one night a week, we should have cooked for her.

My mother didn't finish high school and she didn't read books. But I still remember a day in 1957 when I was eight years old. We were in the kitchen. Something had happened at school. She told me to be strong and stand up for what's right. She said this is called "moral courage."

* * *

At Vancouver Airport I have supper with Peter Barnes, a good friend from grad school. As usual, our conversation ranges from politics to movies to TV.

"If Ally McBeal looked like a bag lady, who would care about her problems?" I ask.

"What's it like for a woman to lose her looks?" I ponder. "Probably like a child discovering she's too old to get special treatment from adults."

Peter is my last link here. After we part, I have a sense of utter loneliness.

Tired from beer and bluster, I have no great expectations for this trip.

In fact, it seems like sheer idiocy. Peter says as much: "How are you going to relate to an 18-year-old you can barely communicate with?"

It's not too late to turn back. But that prospect seems worse than going on.

Why judge by other peoples' standards? Nothing in common? Let's see.

The waiting room is full of Filipinos. They seem like warm people: humble, family oriented. I feel comfortable in their midst.

On the plane, there are no white women. There are a half dozen white men. One is reading *War and Peace*. I wonder if their purpose is the same as mine.

It's a 14-hour flight. As we cruise high above the North Pacific I search for a stance.

All my life I have been like a man facing the rear on a speeding train. I have always had my back to the future. Although the future is unknown, at least now I feel I am facing forward.

Yield. Trust. The sky is full of stars.

* * *

The Philippines strikes me as a country that has been exploited by the West for 400 years and the people are trying to be as good humored about it as possible.

Conquered by the United States in 1902, the Philippines previously had been a colony of Spain for 300 years. Since "independence" in 1946, a few dozen wealthy families have run the country with the support of the CIA.

It's the usual American *modus operandi*. Install a puppet like Ferdinand Marcos who declares the country "open for business."

Filipinos have been trained to treat white people like Afro-Americans once did. All white males are addressed as "Sir". On the plane, a Filipino moved so I could have three seats.

The Philippines is a nation under siege. The have-nots, be they criminals or rebels, besiege the haves. Armed guards protect all businesses from banks to donut shops. Skirmishes are fought daily with Communist or Moslem rebels. The signs at army roadblocks have Pepsi logos.

On the day of my arrival, the big story is the death of the son of a wealthy Chinese magnate. The young man is killed in a shoot-out between kidnappers and police. His wife is pregnant; they were married just six months.

Manila strikes me as a slum with luxury hotels towering above squalid streets choked with traffic and exhaust fumes. I had not yet discovered the rich part of the city, Makati. I make the mistake of visiting the "tourist" section, Ermita.

I am overcome by a pervasive sense of desperation: millions of people struggling to survive and not having much success.

Near the old fort (Intermuros), a tourist site, I see an absolutely beautiful woman with a baby selling 1-cent chewing gum. I want to take her picture but feel like a voyeur.

On a corner, some taxi drivers offer to take me to a place where I can have young girls.

"Too early in the day," I make an excuse.

"You must come first and reserve a girl," they say.

"No, " I dismiss them. "I didn't come here for that."

I came in search of love. Simple me.

But if marrying a foreigner is the only way out for young women here, am I exploiting them too?

Americans are called "Quereros" in Tagalog, literally white devils. Am I a devil too?

I watch street children, a two-year-old child feeding a sucker to his four-year-old brother. In turn, I am observed by a youth who acknowledges my interest with a defeated smile.

I walk for miles searching for somewhere pleasant: coffee shops, art galleries, bookstores. Nothing.

After only a few hours in Manila, I realize I don't want to stay any longer. I can just make the 4 p.m. flight to Davao. I check out of my hotel and head for the airport. The Manila traffic is a Darwinian struggle measured in car lengths.

From the taxi I observe a crumpled figure lying beside the road like a piece of litter. In the steamy afternoon stillness, a bony arm maneuvers a slab of cardboard against the sun.

At the airport, I discover this note on a 10-peso bill in my wallet:
"Wanted
I need a friend
That's all I need."

Two hours later, I am on a modern Airbus 320, high above verdant mountains and azure seas, winging my way south to Davao.

* * *

Life is made up of millions of choices, gambles big and small. At the airport in Davao, someone from *The Insular Century Hotel* greets me. I had read in Manila that the Asia Pacific Beauty Contest was taking place in Davao. "Are the contestants staying at the *Insular*?" I ask their airport man.

No, they are staying at *The Apo View*, he tells me. Nevertheless my guidebook says the *Insular* has 12 acres of grounds, a pool and a private beach. After a day in Manila, I opt for *that*. It's a good decision. It is tasteful, modest and luxurious. And with the fall of the peso, half price.

I have two days to kill before my Tuesday morning rendezvous with Cecilia.

At supper, I spy a dapper-looking white man my age with a beautiful Filipina. Pen pals? I want to compare notes.

Turns out I'm wrong. Brian, 46, who is English, and Clare, 28, have been married six years. They publish city magazines in Manila and are starting one in Davao.

"Most Filipino men don't give a damn about their women," Brian tells me. "They send them to Manila or Hong Kong to be maids or hookers. As long as they send money home, they don't care."

Brian says 80% of Filipino men are this way; Clare says it's more like 50%.

Next day, Gerald, Brian's younger brother tells me: "Brian and his wife moved to Hong Kong from England ten years ago and divorced. Asia is very hard on Western women. Quite simply, they can't compete with Asian women."

Gerald is a photographer who lives in England with his longtime girlfriend. "Guys I know tolerate feminism but they don't like it. Being a man involves certain things." He doesn't elaborate.

He complains about the atmosphere of fear and distrust engendered by feminism. "I can't even smile at a child in a supermarket without being considered a pervert," he says.

* * *

At breakfast next day I talk to Art and Kelly from Los Angeles. He is a retired fireman, 53, with a bushy mustache. She is a traditional woman, 37 but looks 27. Married 15 years, they have been traveling in the East for three months taking pictures of carnivorous plants.

This is his second marriage. He promised to give her kids but when it came time, he couldn't face raising another family. She asked herself if she wanted to look for someone else, and decided no.

Kelly has worked as a secretary since teenage and is now successful in accounting. But Art has a huge pension and she doesn't have to work.

"Feminism gives women options," she says. "To be equal or to be feminine."

She has chosen feminine: "He is my protector. I can't protect him."

Art tells me about the existence of "pheromones", a hormone, which on a cellular level knows if someone would be a suitable sexual partner and mate.

Later, waiting in a line, I overhear Kelly say to Art: "I know you don't want to hear this. But I wish we were home. I miss my bathroom."

Art: "You're right, I don't want to hear that."

* * *

Whenever I see a solitary white male, I assume his purpose is the same as mine. I want to compare notes.

Larry from Omaha is in "security." This is his fifth trip. His first pen pal turned out to have a boyfriend. Then he had a crush on her cousin but *she* didn't want *him*. This trip he'll just cruise the malls.

"I want a girl who is kind, gentle, sweet and loving," he says. "If she's too smart, she'll leave me."

Taxi drivers take him around to neighborhoods to meet marriageable girls. "No luck yet. I guess I'm too picky."

He warns me that many girls are shy and won't talk to you. Others are afraid to leave the Philippines or have boyfriends. He also warns about relatives who descend like locusts. One American had to move and deny his wife all contact with her family.

He is curious about Cecilia. Girls from the provinces are best, he says. They still have morals.

* * *

Although I have flown hundreds of times, I always consider the possibility of the plane crashing. This is my definition of neurosis: always thinking something can go wrong or isn't as it appears. Once, speaking to the pilots after a flight, I marveled that those two tiny engines at the back could propel an airplane this heavy. I could see by their faces that I had unnerved *them!*

But the twin engine Beechcraft carrying me to General Santos City Monday December 8, 1997 is up to the task. I am supposed to meet Cecilia at the airport the next morning. She will be there to meet the flight I was supposed to take from Manila.

A sign near the airport says: "Welcome to South Cotabato: Dole Country." The pineapple not the politician. The taxi driver, Bengi, says between three and 10 white men arrive *every morning* looking for wives. This is depressing. I feel like a spawning salmon.

Do I even want a wife? What if I meet Cecilia and have nothing to say? The dog chases the car. What does he do with it? I have to remind myself: "A man chooses a wife like an Indian chooses a paddle: for love, for children, for company."

What do Filipino men think of white men taking their women? I ask.

"No comment," the cabbie is suddenly political. After a second, he is PR again.

"Good feedback," he says (i.e. the women are happy.)

General Santos is a dusty, bustling fishing and agricultural center of 350,000. Its streets are clogged with brightly painted motorcycles and sidecars called "tricycles". They vie with each other in the crowded streets like little dragons.

I pass on one hotel called "The Concrete Lodge". Instead I go to "The Sydney", a new antiseptic-looking structure. I get a room with a view of an extinct volcano, Mount Matutum, and have supper.

In the dining room, I notice a couple of middle aged white males. They look tired and used up. In my room, I ask myself: Am I like them? I must be out of my mind. It's night. I'm tired and alone in a hotel room 8500 miles from home. I don't know a soul.

* * *

How did I get to this place? It started in May 1997 when I was visiting my father in Ottawa. He has a Filipino housekeeper named "Dolly". In her mid thirties, she is pleasant and very attractive. She must have been unbelievable when she was younger. She is married to a Canadian whom she met through a correspondence club.

"Dolly," I asked. "How did you choose your husband from all the men who wrote?"

She answered: "He was the first to visit me in the Philippines."

I liked these odds. Ever since the movie, *Mutiny on the Bounty,* I've had a vision of beautiful bare-breasted tropical island women, adoring and submissive. Could this paradise still exist?

From Ottawa, I went to Toronto where I stayed with my brother. Leafing through back issues of *Toronto Life,* I came across an ad for the "Canadian Correspondence Club." They offered pictures and descriptions of one thousand women from the Philippines and Russia for $5.

When the catalogue arrived, the descriptions of the Filipinas struck me with the force of a revelation. Here were many beautiful young women in their early twenties willing to consider husbands as old as 60. I was a youthful 47.

They seemed to be standard issue for male veterans of our sex wars. Ranging from 5 foot to 5'5" and weighing about 100-110 lbs., they have no complicated interests or demands. Generic women, they described themselves as "simple" and like reading, cooking, music and movies. They were all looking for a man who was "loyal, loving, understanding." One wrote: "Looks, age and money are not important. Honesty, fidelity, character and a sweet loving nature are."

"Filipinas simply do not look at a man's age the way North American women do," the catalogue read. "She will look for leadership. She will look for mentoring. She will look for a secure, sincere, devoted, home life . . .She is a team player."

"Although the Filipina has been brought up to serve her husband and family, she fully expects you to consult with her. She is not a slave and will not accept being a toy. She needs to have agreed and significant responsibility. However the husband is head of the household and has the final word."

I sent away for their addresses, which cost $80. I drafted a letter saying I was looking for a traditional woman who is loving, intelligent, graceful and funny and sent it to 16 women ranging in age from 20 to 38. I got only four replies. Two were from sisters of the women I wrote. (Their sisters were married. Would I consider them?) The other two were from the extremes of the age spectrum. The 38-year-old was now 41 and her picture didn't grab me.

That left the 20 year old, Cecilia. Except she admitted she was really 18.

"Hello from the Philippines! I am pleased to know you...surprised as well.

Just can't express by words how joyful I am to encounter such life's surprise. It's been a long time that I sent an application ... and I didn't expect to get a response anymore."

She had been a university student but had to quit for lack of funds. She described herself as "open, straight forward, communicative, cheerful, easy to get along with, possess a wonderful sense of humor. Having a wide range of interests, and of course know a little about a lot of topics." But she cautioned me, "I am simple in nature, adventurer with a little touch of arts."

In my reply, I asked many questions about our age difference and why Filipinas want to marry western men. Here is her reply.

"I'm willing to consider a man so much older than me 'coz first there's no problem (for me) 'bout the age the important thing is we are compatible. Can handle problems situations well 'coz the one who is older than me will understand me for my shortcomings and can understand that life is not all about happiness. Honestly, there are so many Filipino girls who want to go abroad .. with different reasons, some because of self interests (opportunistic-beware that kind of woman). Some want to have a job 'coz of circumstances –financial problems—wanting to help their loved ones."

I asked her what kind of wife she would be, and what she was looking for in a husband.

" Surely I will not be the perfect wife (nobody is perfect) but I'll be an honest, loving and responsible wife to her husband, a kind of wife that will give importance to her family's reputation, that could understand her husband even to his short comings, will support her husband in all

aspects, strong enough to face challenges/trials that will come to the family. Yet, the qualities of husband I'm looking for are God fearing, honest, can love/accept me for what I am. Same as me could face trials, strong enough. and of course a husband that will live with me "forever" w/ my children 'coz I don't want broken family. I know children will be the one that's affected when parents got separated. '

She sent me a tiny picture of herself. On long autumn nights, I would look at it with a magnifying glass. This girl is as attractive as any I've seen, I concluded.

* * *

In my hotel room, I look at myself in the mirror. Cecilia won't want you. You are too fat and ugly. I suck in my cheeks. You're washed up. Finished.

I go to bed but toss and turn. Finally I get up, pour some Scotch and turn on the TV. The markets are open in New York and all my stock options are way up. I am up $50,000. *You're a genius*, I tell myself.

I spend the next hour trying to get through to my broker. I want to buy more. The access number advertised by my phone company isn't working yet. I am mad enough to sue. God is protecting me. The stocks all tanked from there.

The whiskey takes effect. I am most lucid when I am drunk. I depend on being inebriated in one form or another for *Truth*:

What's wrong with sexual relations today is that men cannot be dominant. If I cannot be dominant in a relationship, I don't want it.

Why should I feel guilty about wanting to rule my own roost? Feminists have brainwashed us with crazy notions of equality. What does equality, a political and economic concept, have to do with love? Love is about self-surrender.

It's not about Cecilia wanting me. It's whether I want her. If she doesn't want me, someone else will.

To those who object to my loving a much younger woman:

A man's freedom to love is the most sacred freedom of all. You can't dictate what will take his breath away. You can't tell his heart when to leap.

* * *

After about three hours of sleep, I arrive at the airport early hoping to take some pictures of Cecilia before she recognizes me.

But I can't find her and before I know it, a rather plain looking girl, much darker than I expected, someone I wouldn't have noticed or recognized, introduces herself to me.

"Hendry? I am Cecilia."

I am disappointed with her appearance and I am afraid she can tell. I am also disappointed that she has a chaperon, her Aunt Veronica, 24.

I switch into blind date mode: be friendly, confirm the first impression, and then politely extricate myself. We get a taxi and head for town. I had been warned that Filipinas are shy but I am not prepared for this.

Cecilia won't answer any of my questions. She covers her face and acts stumped and embarrassed. Her aunt in the front seat volunteers that Ceci was so nervous about meeting me, she didn't sleep all night.

"Do you like me?" I ask. No answer.

"Well I like you," I say in an effort to make her more comfortable. The details of "Plan B" float across my mind. Good thing I wrote to other girls in Devao. Flight back 7.45 tomorrow morning.

"Where do you want to go now?" I ask. " What do you want to do?"

Then she says those three magic words I have been waiting a lifetime to hear:

"*You're the boss.*"

I suggest we go to the Sydney Hotel for lunch *without* Auntie. But when we arrive, Cecilia is in such emotional disarray I ask if she wants Veronica along. She signals "yes" with a flick of her eyebrows.

At lunch, I have to focus my conversation on Veronica because Cecilia won't talk to me. Cecilia is painfully self-conscious, especially about a tooth that is discolored and another that is crooked.

Veronica is a nurse who looks after workers at an asparagus packing plant. She earns $3-4 U.S. a day, about the same as the workers.

"What kinds of ailments do you treat?" I ask.

"Colds and headaches," she replies evasively.

I decide that pictures of my family might help break the ice with

Cecilia. I go upstairs to my hotel room. I don't take the ones of my house. They will not be necessary.

"This is a disaster," I think as I wait for the elevator. "Thank God I took the precaution of writing to other women. How to get away?"

When I arrive back at the table, Ceci has two pictures of her own. She pushes them across the table. One shows an absolutely beautiful girl.

"This is *you*?" I am astonished. I am sitting opposite her and can't believe I am looking at the same girl.

"When was it taken?"

A week ago.

In the cab I had noticed that Cecilia seemed to be carrying an emotional burden.

Was it just lack of sleep and anxiety? Her face seemed haggard, stern, much older than her 18 years. Why?

Looking at pictures of my family and friends, Ceci blurts out: "You must come to Maitum."

I like this sign of initiative. What have I got to lose? I agree.

We go to a supermarket to buy food. Ceci asks if I like orange juice, and puts some flavor crystals in the cart. I put them back on the shelf. We are in the plantation capital of the world and she's buying flavor crystals.

"I eat real food," I tell her. She drifts off to another section.

Have I hurt her feelings? Never apologize.

She is holding some canned beans. I put them away.

"I'll eat what you eat."

Communication is mostly facial. No words.

"Do you want me to go back for tomatoes?"

She looks at me. I can tell she wants me to. She doesn't have to flick her eyebrows. I try to imagine what silent nagging might be like.

We head for the terminal to wait for the van to Maitum. Waiting there, a couple-like coordination develops as we manage our bags and jockey for place. She picks some lint from my arm. I like that.

We sit together in the front of the new VW van that makes the 2-hour trip. The driver puts on my cassette of Van Morrison's *Avalon Sunset*.

The scenery starts to change. Bright sunlight. Panoramic ocean and mountain views. Outriggers pulled up on white sandy beaches lined by coconut trees. Villages of thatched houses on stilts. Farmers behind oxen ploughing rice paddies. Your standard western vision of paradise.

Inspirational melodies in my ears, breathtaking panoramas in my eyes, and Ceci's soft body in my arm, things are improving fast.

Indeed, I am ready to marry her. There may be prettier girls here. But I want this one. Get your head examined! Are you desperate? Or crazy? Is it pheromones?

But as long as I have my arm around her, this is how I feel. I am tired of being single. I am tired of the lonely circus that has been my romantic life. I am ready to take a wife. And this girl seemed ready too.

We arrive in Maitum, a town of about 8,000 and take a tricycle to Ceci's home. I am relieved that her father, Andy, is much older than me. He could have been younger.

The family's home is an eye opener. It resembles a large (1800 square feet) split level shed. It has a concrete floor and walls, wooden slat windows, and corrugated tin roof. There are benches and a table but no furniture. There is electricity but no running water. The toilet is in the backyard along with a rooster and two pigs. It is the sit-on-your-honches variety you flush yourself. The stove is a one-burner charcoal fire.

Ceci shows me her room. It is upstairs and has a nice wooden floor. I sit down on her bed and am surprised to discover it has no mattress.

"You don't have a mattress?"

"I am used to it."

Her parents sleep on mats on the floor in the next room. I ask her father why as a handyman, he doesn't make a mattress.

"I don't have the capital," he replies.

This is a man who has worked hard all his life and basically has nothing. The house, I learn later, belongs to the church, which is over the backyard wall. They live there rent-free in exchange for upkeep.

Cecilia's mother, Mely, works next door as housekeeper/child sitter for the wealthy neighbor who runs a rice and coconut wholesale operation called a "buy and sell." Mely works 11-hour days and makes 40 pesos a day, about $1 U.S. ($1.50 before the devaluation). Andy says he makes 4000 peso a month, about $100, but some months fall short. The pigs belong to the neighbor.

Coming from a continent where the cry of the heart is, "*Where should I invest?*" it is sobering to live with people who have almost no money.

I take over buying the food.

Ceci is not deprived of clothes. That's where money is spent: T-shirts, jeans, sarongs, and dresses. But she doesn't have a tape deck or any music. There is a radio downstairs.

Also downstairs is the display of Cecilia's beauty queen trophies and ribbons. The ribbons have inscriptions like "Miss Photogenic – 2nd Place". Prominent is the "Miss Malalag 1997" trophy. (Malalag is the county.)

I am anxious to see the beach. When we get there, Cecilia's silence is unnerving. She ignores many of my questions and doesn't ask any. But she listens intently when I tell her about myself and her face expresses warmth and interest.

"You look older than your years. Did something bad happen?" No answer.

"Why don't you talk to me?" No answer.

"When will you talk to me? In five years? How will I know if I love you?"

No answer.

She plays in the waves while I sulk on the beach. I am reminded of the avoidance games lovers play. As we wend our way back, among the colorful catamarans pulled up on the sand, I am ready to give up.

Let some other man pay to fix her teeth, I fume.

"Look Ceci. If I put your new picture in the Canadian Correspondence Club catalogue, you'll have 100 pen pals. They'll build a hotel to accommodate them. You'll drive the economy."

Silence.

That evening two of her father's cronies come by. Actually they are senior members of the Catholic congregation who helped Andy get this house.

I ask them if Filipinas are normally so unresponsive.

"Traditionally, the Filipina is shy in courtship," one replies. "She is reserved. My wife didn't talk to me until I courted her for three months."

I have three weeks.

* * *

There is no hotel in Maitum; I am to stay with the rich neighbors. But I indicate a preference for Ceci's hard bed and suggest she sleep with the neighbors since she knows them. Instead she sleeps with her parents in the next room on the floor.

I am exhausted and don't have trouble sleeping. But there is no snooze button in a farming community. At about 5 a.m., the roosters start crowing and the chorus reverberates for miles. Later I discover eight roosters in an adjacent yard. No wonder I'm getting it in stereo.

The next day we go to swim at a scenic waterfall 10 km away. We take a tricycle and then hike on a road bordered by rice paddies. Later, Andy tells me that he was afraid I would be kidnapped by the Islamic Liberation Army.

I am trying to make Cecilia talk. My questions elicit only short answers or silence. "Do you want to go to America?" Nothing. " Do you go to movies?" Yes. "Last movie seen?" She can't remember. "Last book read?" Silence.

This can't work. Yet, she seems to talk and laugh in her native language with her family and friends …

Two adolescent boys are swimming at the falls. There is also a hose hooked up to the flow. Cecilia and the boys spray each other with it, splashing and squealing.

Later, lying on a flat rock, she lets me hold her again. Simple man, that makes up for a lot.

On the hike back, I devise a game that gets us talking. I teach her English vocabulary. I choose words beginning from A to Z and ask her to define and spell them. Some of the choices are pointed.

"B" is for bashful. "That's what you are."

"C" is for candid. She knows the meaning and spelling.

(Incidentally English is Cecilia's sixth language. She speaks Tagalog and five local dialects including some Arabic.)

Are you candid? I ask her.

"What do you think?" she replies.

I don't think she is, in the western sense of saying everything you think and feel.

But I can't say she isn't. Her face. Her actions. They also speak. So I say, "Yes, you are candid."

The game establishes a rapport. Her face becomes animated and beautiful.

When we get back, I lie on her hard bed waiting for her to return to my arms. But she doesn't. Instead she sits at the foot of the bed drawing. I feel ignored.

After a while, I pull her to me but she resists. My mood sours. I begin to brood.

She doesn't like me, after all. This isn't about *love.* It's about *poverty.*

With so many beautiful women in the Philippines, why am I wasting my time here?

"I think I will leave tomorrow," I taunt her.

No response.

"Do you want me to go?"

She shakes her head with feeling. I decide to write her a note.

"Ceci, when you don't want to hug me, it says to me that you don't really like me, and I should go. I want to find a girl who really likes me as I like her. I don't want to waste your time and mine."

She studies the note, turns it over, and begins to write. We are pen pals again.

"Henry, Remember we are staying in my parents' house. I respect them 'coz they're conservative.

Filipino people are very different from you. I want to hug you but as I said, we have to respect my parents. If you want to find another girl I have nothing to do with that—the decision is yours."

"I don't want another girl," I say. "I thought you didn't like me."

I have to get her out of her parents' home. I pen another note:

" Ceci, would you be willing to come with me to a beautiful hotel with

outdoor pool in Devao. We would stay together but in separate beds and I would not ask more of you than hugging."

She likes this idea, but she needs her father's permission. I am encouraged once more.

"Ceci, do you like me? I need to hear it."

She raises her eyebrows.

"I like you very much," I say.

She covers my eyes with her hand.

* * *

Cecilia has a bad cough. She starts coughing, then has to go outside and spit. I had had a similar condition but it was in remission. I ask her why she doesn't go to a doctor. The doctor is free but there is no money for medicine.

I take her to the local hospital, which sports the banner: "This is a Breast Feeding Hospital." There is a dog lounging in the lobby and a frog makes its way down the hall. There are small lizards on the walls but otherwise everything seems efficient.

Dr. "Junie", a charming woman in her 30's, congratulates me on nabbing "Miss Maitum 1997."

"All women are beautiful here," I say.

She summons a half dozen midwives and nurses in their 20's. "This is my staff. Can you find them husbands? Someone like you. So handsome; so young-looking; Cecilia, where did you find him?"

"And you Dr. Junie, don't you want a husband?" I ask. She is married and has three young children.

I take the women's information for the Canadian Correspondence Club. They even have pictures handy. "Why do so many Filipinas want to marry foreigners?" I ask Dr. Junie.

Her tone is adamant. "Number One. The men here are indigent. They only earn 3000 pesos a month (around $90 U.S.) They can't give women and their children a good future."

"Number two. Because of the army, deaths in the ongoing civil war, the ratio of women to men is four to one."

I ask about the ratio of male and female births. She says it is 3-2 in favor of females.

Dr. Junie listens to Celia's back with a stethoscope and prescribes.

Afterward, Cecilia and I go to the outdoor market to buy food for supper.

Everyone stares at us. I am the only white man in town. I suddenly appreciate how a celebrity feels, never being anonymous.

Except this has an edge to it. Here is the town beauty queen cavorting with a white man who can break her out of the poverty prison. We are the objects of intense curiosity.

* * *

From *Insight Philippines:* The Filipina: From Priestesses Descended

Once daughter and consort to proud, free men, she became an adopted waif to be melded in the Castilian mold. The friar who was father figure to whole villages fancied her a naïve child, tenderheartedly teaching her his alphabet…The fervor with which she once worshipped nature and ancestral spirits was rechannelled now to Christian piety…

Bound now and "saved" from former joyous abandon to the juices of life, the solemn young thing with all her thoughts on chastity became a tempting morsel. Over and over again and much to her trauma, the Filipina was seduced by her good father . . .

These indiscretions caused a subtle fissure in tribal life. Friar children, though illegitimate, enjoyed a slightly higher status as Castilian progeny….To be white became the object of many a silent prayer for the next generation. To find a rich handsome Spaniard to marry became the goal for which many daughters were whipped when they played too long in the sun. The hang-up against a sun tan lasts to this day.

The effect on the Filipino male was devastating. Battered by forced labor and exorbitant taxes, he found his status even more galling when wife or daughter was raped by a powerful Spaniard. There was no recourse except perhaps in drink, and many a young Filipina grew up only to be torn between her own longing for a better life and her father's wounded and festering pride.

* * *

Back home, I make supper.

"Women should never cook," I quip to Andy. "They should be kept, like cats."

Cecilia is not amused. Joanne, a friend of Cecilia's, is a guest for supper. Joanne mentions she had a pen pal but sent him packing.

Why?

"I've always had a vocation," she replies sweetly. "I want to be a nun."

She has the determined jaw of a nun. "What will you do as a nun?" I ask. "Teach?"

"I want to help beggars and street kids. My heart goes out to them."

"I too was called," I confess. "Called but *not* chosen. Actually, it was a wrong number. God asked for a Bruce. Sorry God just me here. He hung up." Everyone laughs. They never miss anything funny.

"Many are called but few are chosen," Joanne repeats. "But do you *believe* in Jesus Christ?"

"Yes."

"Do you believe in God? "

"I don't believe. I *know*," I answer.

Andy also affirms his belief. "God has given me everything I have." He is grateful.

"Perhaps you will be God's instrument for Andy's situation," Joanne says.

"Yes," I agree. "Certainly for Ceci and she is God's instrument for me."

I have already fallen for her. She doesn't talk to me but her soul creates a light show on her face. It is a beautiful soul: sweet, loving, and vivid. I am in love with her soul.

During supper, she passes me a note:

Henry, I already talked to my father and he said I will not be going w/ you alone in Devao City. I must have a companion w/ me or w/ us. I told you the tradition of Filipino people is very different. For us, Filipina, will take care of herself in order to take care also of her family's name. (Reputation is very important.) I hope you can understand me as I should obey my parents. They are just taking care of me. Anyway, how long will it take to stay there? The only option is bringing a companion w/ me (maybe a friend) to be with you. I want to be with you but not alone to respect also my parents and I know it's for my own good. I hope you can understand 'coz for us Filipina should not go with a man or a guy alone (not good).

I scan the letter quickly. I quickly compromise on the chaperon.

Who will we take? Cecilia nods in Joanne's direction.

Joanne welcomes the opportunity. But she needs her guardian's permission. Her guardian is her grandfather, Maximo, a retired rice farmer in his 80's.

After supper, we visit him. This man, who is going blind and senile, holds my romantic destiny in his hands. Surrounded by his large extended family and friends, I have to prove I am not a recruiter for a Hong Kong brothel.

I introduce the situation: I am Cecilia's pen pal; we have Andy's permission to go to a wonderful hotel in Devao, but only with a chaperon.

"How do I know you will return Joanne?" Maximo asks.

"Return Joanne? I *don't want* her. I'm only interested in Cecilia."

"You have only been here a few days. I don't know your habit and character." He asks about my occupation and family.

"Will your baggage remain at Andy's?"

Yes, I lie. I'm not sure I won't move on from Devao.

"I want to suggest that you take along Joanne's uncle."

"A chaperon for the chaperon? That doesn't make sense. Should I take your whole family? We just won't go."

Joanne is grinning. Ceci is embarrassed.

"You will have separate rooms?" Maximo retreats a little.

"Separate rooms floors apart. Separate keys. Complete privacy," I assure him.

I make a final, heartfelt appeal.

"Maximo. I am an honorable man. I am very fond of Cecilia. I only want the best for Joanne and Cecilia. Sometimes you have to *trust*. I am taking a risk too. I have to trust that Cecilia really loves me and not what I can give her."

Maximo gives his assent.

Jubilant, we retreat to Cecilia's house.

Andy and Celle and I have a coke.

"I trust you," Andy says.

"I trust you too," I say.

Celle: "We all have to trust."

Celle leaves us alone.

"I am too old to fool around," I tell Andy. "I love Cecilia and want to make her happy. I'll take good care of her. I have already bought her medicine."

"I am poor," Andy says.

"You have dignity."

"Thanks," he says.

Then he adds:

"Maximo suggests that I go with you."

"Celle needs her freedom. She won't let me kiss her."

"I understand," he concedes.

* * *

The next morning Joanne, Cecilia and I take the van to General Santos.

I make the mistake of getting us dropped at the airport 10 kms from town. Our flight to Devao isn't till 4 p.m. and I want to check the bags. But there are no taxis back to town. We wonder around forlornly (while I curse my stupidity) until finally we hitch a ride with two airline mechanics.

After buying our tickets, we are practically the only customers at a gaudy upscale restaurant. The waiters look surly but the food is good.

Cecilia turns her nose up at a taste of my steak. I ask her for some of her vegetables and look for signs of her generosity. She isn't generous even though she doesn't finish her dish.

We kill time in the dusty city park. The temperature is about 95 F. I am getting sick of people staring at us. I swear I am not coming back to this city again. I'm moving on from Devao.

We kill more time later in the air-conditioned airport waiting room. Cecilia's silence is unnerving me again. "Is Cecilia always this quiet?" I ask Joanne.

"Yes," her friend says in saintly tones. "She is simple, quiet, good."

Do I have to bring Joanne to talk to?

I think I am going to die because Cel is shy. DIE/SHY. I can't stand the silence.

Cecilia senses my frustration. When I cough, she pounds my chest. She mentions a massage in Devao. She seems to be saying, "I'll look after you, not your intellectual needs, but *you*."

Can this work? Is it she a geisha? A full time concubine? Am I buying her? Is that it?

I have a brochure for the game *Lovers and Liars*. To pass time, I ask Cecilia one of the questions.

"*If your lover had a nightmare and couldn't sleep, would you want him to wake you up for comfort?*"

"It is my obligation," she says. "My duty."

"Well I hope you would also be motivated by love," I say priggishly.

Another question: "*You hit it off with someone at a party. Your lover seems jealous. Do you cut your conversation short?*"

Joanne answers that, as a "professional, independent woman," she would not.

Cecilia says she would interrupt the conversation to explain to her lover that he had nothing to worry about.

Another question: "*Basking in the glow after fabulous sex, you realize you're starving. Do you jump up to make a sandwich?*"

This reduces both girls to giggles. Dejected, I go and sit by myself.

By the time we get to Devao, my mood has worsened. I am tired of the traveling, the staring, the waiting and the heat. I leave Cecilia and Joanne to wrestle with their baggage while I stride on ahead. Finally a porter helps them.

It is not my finest moment. My mood is black. *Only a miracle will make me go back to Maitum on Monday.*

I have a beautiful room with a view of the pool. I take a shower, put on clean clothes and relax. There is only one thing that can make me feel better. Holding Cecilia in my arm. I knock on the girls' door.

There is a disconcerting wait before they open.

It's already late and they're in bed. The TV is blaring. Their clothes are strewn about. It has all the trappings of a pajama party.

Lying in bed, Joanne's face has a soft glow. Her chin is less pronounced. I wonder if I chose the right one. Joanne *talks*.

Stay the course. I mention the massage to Cecilia.

"Bye and bye," she says (i.e. later).

A vision flashes through my mind: I take two girls to a luxury hotel for four days and Cecilia will have nothing to do with me. I brood in solitude by the pool, reading newspapers while the girls watch MTV in their room and ridicule me. My male conditioning is speaking.

"My room Cecilia," I say. She hesitates.

"Go with him," Joanne coaxes her.

To my immense relief, she comes with me.

Soon she is lying beside me on my king-size bed. Only she is hugging a pillow.

She is really shy. She's never been with a man like this.

"You don't have to love me," I assure her. "I can be like a brother if we don't love one other romantically. "

"I don't want to have sex," I tell her. "I wouldn't harm you for anything in the world."

I tell her that when a man loves a woman, he wants to nurture her and see her strong and happy.

"Your love and trust mean more to me than anything. I won't do anything to jeopardize them," I say.

She is listening, holding her pillow.

"Why does that pillow deserve your hugs?" I ask. "Does it tell you how beautiful you are? Does it buy you medicine when you're sick? Does it want to love you?"

After a while, I am holding and kissing her. I am calm and happy. She is beautiful. We stare into each other's eyes.

The phone rings.

It is Joanne inquiring if she can phone an uncle in Manila who is supporting her but hasn't sent a check. Go ahead. Don't bother us.

Hugging again. Kissing. Even some talking. Things are going very well when the phone rings again. Joanne?!

No! It's one of the girls from Plan B! *She wasn't supposed to phone! She was supposed to write!*

I can't talk now. I say. But the girl, a Gwendolyn, insists on giving me her phone number which, needless to say, I don't write down. "I will wait for you to call," she says.

I hang up. Immediately I tell Cecilia who it is. I explain about "Plan B."

Cecilia is very upset. She clams up. I plead with her. I try to take her into my arms again. But her soft body has become a steel coil. She won't be moved.

"What was I supposed to do if I didn't like you or if you didn't like me? I know you have other pen pals. I saw a letter from France in your room."

No response. I can't understand her behavior. I am being forthright. And it doesn't help. "Maybe I should have lied to you?"

Nothing. Finally I get angry. "If you can't recognize an honest man, you don't deserve one."

She starts to budge. I am relieved to see her rummaging for pen and paper. After what seems like a lifetime, she hands me a note.

Tell me who's that girl? Is she living here in Davao City? The reason why you didn't (take) the flight to Gen San City last Dec. 9 (Tues. 7.30 a.m.) Did you meet her before you went to Gen.San? I want you to tell me the truth.—

I *really* liked the jealous tone. And *suspicious!*

I tell her the truth: I had only written that girl. Anyone at the hotel could confirm I had been alone. You are Plan A. That girl was Plan B.

Soon this storm has passed and we are petting up another one.

* * *

Breakfast next day is buffet style. Cecilia asks me to get her food and I oblige. I wait on her scrupulously, telling her in this way what she means to me. Eating in silence, I scorn western lovers who have to chat constantly to reassure each other they have rapport.

After breakfast, she complains of a backache. I give her a massage in my room, and soon we are making out again.

She gives me all the loving I could ask for, given our level of commitment. I did not expect this. I am blissful.

Her love is the ultimate reason I fall for her. She *trusts*. She *receives*. *She makes the leap of faith*. She takes the big gamble. In my experience, western women are *so* calculating with their love.

Cecilia surrenders to my kisses and caresses wholeheartedly. I have never seen such love as in her eyes, such tenderness as in her face. I have been searching for this all my life.

I can tell she loves me and is not trying to escape her economic situation. I have been with prostitutes. I know the difference. And I am not her only eligible suitor.

I worry about the silence. But later, in her room, I come across a note in one of my books. She hasn't given it to me.

Henry, I am (little) quiet at first. But you will find me humorous. Just give me a time, OK? As I said to you, Filipina is very different. I have to adjust. We are only together for how many days and I did not go before with a man if I'll just meet him for only a few days.

It's only been four days since she was awkwardly covering her face in the taxi from the airport.

"Will you obey your husband if he is just and good?" I ask her.

"Yes," she replies.

The talk will come later.

* * *

Is this what I want? I ask myself. Yes.

But what about all the other Filipinas? How could you choose the *first* one?

The women here are so beautiful, doe-like and willing. Many return my glance.

There is a palpable feminine heat in this country. I could find a dozen wives.

But love is a passionate not a rational activity. I am not going to conduct interviews and make a short list. Besides, I'd rather spend my vacation making love to one girl, and beginning a life with her, than interviewing ten.

Cecilia is asleep on my bed. She can finally sleep because she knows I am hers.

Afterward we walk by the beach.

"Will you ever get tired of my kisses?" I ask.

Without hesitation: "No."

* * *

I lunch by myself in the hotel restaurant. Cloying Christmas carols are playing. Scattered about, white imperialists meet with their Filipino underlings.

I read the headline in the Herald Tribune: "World Markets Down: New Surge of Panic Hits South Korea." There is a picture with caption: "Worried investor phones broker as riot police stand by."

I have money in the markets but I don't care. Money no longer drives my life. Until now I have been addicted to playing the market. I couldn't quit because there was nothing else to value above money. Not my health, or my happiness and sanity. Every morning, the fickle fluctuations of the market affected my mood. I had no peace of mind.

My love for Cecilia has given me something more important. I'm free at last.

* * *

Later, another girl from "Plan B" phones while Cecilia and Joanne are in the room. This girl, an "Elenita", sounds very charming but I am prepared this time. I tell her I have met a young woman and I am in love.

She doesn't seem to understand. She repeats that she would be glad to meet me. I tell her I am already involved and hang up.

Cecilia seems satisfied and this interruption causes no repercussions. I disconnect the phone.

Before supper, Cecilia and I have a drink and we are reflective for the first time.

She asks, "What did you think of my first letter?" I can't remember it.

I ask what did you think of my letters? She says she'll tell me one day.

Not exactly sparkling repartee but at least we are talking.

I ask what she thought when I wrote that I could only promise her one child. She says her reaction was, well at least he'll have one.

How many would she want?

Two. I am in a mood to have ten.

I ask, "What did you think of me at the airport on the first day?"

"It's a secret," she says. Later she confesses that I looked younger than she expected.

We talk about what she'll do in Canada. She says she'll get a job so she can support her parents.

I make a joke about eating the noisy roosters for Xmas dinner. "Have you ever killed a chicken?" I ask.

"Yes, a few times, " she says. "And plucked their feathers."

How did you like that?

She enjoyed it.

Do you fetch water?

Everyday.

I make a mental note: Never marry a woman who doesn't fetch water and know how to kill and pluck a chicken.

Chapter Two

⬚

Love is a Journey

Love is a journey, I tell Cecilia at supper. I feel as if I am beginning a long journey. Tears well up in my eyes. I can hardly contain my happiness.

The hotel is fully booked and the girls have to move in with me after only one night. Joanne sleeps on the couch.

I am filled with love for the girl sleeping beside me. In repose, her face looks so brown, so exotic. Waves of affection tumble over me. I am afraid of making a fool of myself.

How will this story go? I want it to move forward. Cecilia will only emerge in the context of commitment. I want to give her that.

I want to get engaged. I want to exchange rings. I want to consecrate myself to her. It's an act of faith. Faith always precedes action. I am not afraid of making mistakes. They are rarely fatal.

* * *

At breakfast Saturday I outline the plan to Joanne in Cecilia's presence. Ceci and I will get engaged. We will buy rings today. Joanne will return to Maitum alone on Monday and explain to Andy that his daughter is engaged, that she is safe, that she will remain a virgin until we are married.

Joanne will explain that Henry can't stand the staring in Maitum, that we need some time and some space.

Suddenly I realize that I have not even consulted Cecilia.

"Will you agree to become engaged?"

Her eyebrows indicate yes.

My heart leaps with a bound I feel down to my loins.

"Do you agree to stay here alone with me? You know I'll respect your wishes."

She is silent. She weighs her father's reaction against my own aversion to going back to Maitum. She factors in her own desires. She remains silent. It means she agrees to stay.

"Do you love me?" I ask.

"Of course," she answers in a reproachful tone.

* * *

After breakfast, we take a taxi to the mall to buy the ring.

Cecilia is a chameleon. When we are alone together, her face is all love. But in the mall, surrounded by crowds, it is plain, impersonal, practical. She chooses a ring as if she were buying shoes.

Irrationally, I start to question her love. *Insecurity about love is my craziness.* I just feel shut out.

On the way back to the hotel, my mind spins out of control. Is this an elaborate hoax? Marry the rich white sap and look after the relatives? I feel like a senile child caught with his hand in the cookie jar of life. What right do I have to grasp happiness?

Joanne wants to visit the local orphanage. We stop at a convent to find out where the orphanage is. A nun greets us. Both girls' faces glow in her presence. At one time Cecilia also wanted to become a nun.

Turns out the orphanage is miles from town. I ask the nun for directions to a Buddhist monastery mentioned in the guidebook.

Disdain on her face, the nun points with a limp finger.

I pick up on her attitude: "Do you and the other nuns like to party with the monks?"

"We have our own recreation here," she replies primly.

* * *

Back in the hotel room, Cecilia is teasing me. Still sore from my anxiety attack, I ask Joanne to leave. "Cecilia is mean to me when you are here. She is nice when we are alone."

The decision to get engaged proves to be the right one. That afternoon we do move forward. As part of her sexual initiation, I plan to introduce a few lessons. Instead we skip many grades. The decision to hold off intercourse until marriage becomes problematic.

After, I suffer the bewilderment of someone who gets everything he wants.

I have a feeling of abundance. *I can't take any more.*

* * *

I sit alone in the open-air lobby of the hotel puffing a cigarillo and savoring the moment.

How much of what I say states what should be *obvious* if it is real. "Was it good for you too?" "Do you love me?" *Why do I have to verbalize everything before it's real?* I must be unreal.

I plot the realpolitik of this huge reservoir of beautiful young women eager for western men. The next step in globalization is to make North American women compete with Asian women, which they can't.

Basically American women are in the position of big labor in the seventies: spoiled, arrogant and egotistical. *They have forgotten how to love.* The answer is to flood the market with millions of lithe, loving Asian beauties.

Puffing my cigar, I look at the other beautiful young women working at the hotel.

I regret I can make only one happy. Before calamity comes pride.

* * *

The evening of my first day as an engaged man begins well. I give Cecilia a beautiful pearl necklace and bracelet as an engagement present. (They are produced locally and aren't as expensive as they sound.)

My reward is Cecilia's expression when she sees the pearls and her regal appearance wearing them. She doesn't rave or prattle on about how beautiful they are.

Then we play *Scruples* and Cecilia starts to get on my nerves.

Sometimes she speaks with a childish whine, which in her accent drives me crazy. "My cards no good, you no fair" she keeps whining.

When I can take no more of this, I ask Joanne to give us some time alone again.

"You ask me to take my elbows off the table because it's not attractive," I tell Cecilia. "Will you promise to stop whining? It's very unattractive. I love you so much; I can't stand not liking you."

She agrees. I say I'll change for her too.

The next issue is her washing her hair. The previous night we had to wait up for hours while it dried. I admit I had an ulterior motive. I just got engaged. I wanted to hold her.

I ask her to wash her hair in the morning.

No, she wants to wash it now.

"I bought you pearls. The least you can do is wash your hair in the morning." I stupidly say.

"Blackmail!" she cries.

"I'll divorce you." I threaten. Why stop at stupid?

"That's up to you," she replies, rolling her eyes and making faces of exasperation and anger. Silence.

I can't stand it. "OK. Go ahead and wash you hair."

"No," she says.

"Please smile. Please. I can't stand being apart."

Finally she relents.

"You are a bird in a nest in my tree. I adore you."

* * *

But our problems for the night aren't over.

Joanne comes back and they watch TV. At 11 p.m. I want to go to bed. "Lights out, it's time for sleep,"

In the dark, I want to cuddle before drifting off. Cecilia doesn't oblige.

"Hendree, it's time for sleep," she says in that grating whine.

I'm convinced she's teasing me, using my *exact* words, punishing me for turning off the TV. I keep trying, but she keeps saying: "Hendree, it's time for sleep."

It seems so unjust to refuse to cuddle on the night of our engagement.

"Cecilia, what did I do to be treated like this? We got engaged. I bought you that necklace."

"Hendree, do you want me to give back your pearls?"

Jesus. This seems so unfair. I had asked her not to tease me. And here she is killing me. I turn over in disgust: "You're full of crap," I mutter.

After a few minutes, she goes to the bathroom and doesn't return. About 15 minutes later, I push my way in (the door is unlocked). She is sitting on the floor with her writing pad looking very distraught.

"Are you writing to me?"

No, she is writing a friend. This is bad. I beg her to tell me what had gone wrong, why she put me off. No answer.

She struggles with the clasp of her pearls. I help her remove them. First she gives back the necklace, then the bracelet.

"This is why I never accept gifts from my suitors. They try to blackmail me."

I plead with her to explain why she had resisted me. I try to take her in my arms but her body is in steel coil mode. Suddenly my dream seems to be falling apart.

This girl is as neurotic as women in America. My past comes welling up. I feel as though I have spent my whole life on a cold bathroom floor begging some crazy woman to tell me what I have done wrong.

My sister accused me of pursuing a ridiculous fantasy, and at that moment she seems right. Cecilia is another neurotic teenager. Suddenly, with an eerie clarity, I see myself as others must: a foolish middle aged man engaged to a child.

I have been going 70 mph and have hit a brick wall. I am dazed. I can get nothing out of Cecilia so I wake Joanne. "You must talk to Cecilia, she is acting crazy."

After conferring on the balcony, Joanne returns and says Cecilia will talk to me.

Cecilia says the sex thing has been too fast, too much.

She wasn't teasing me. It dawns on me that the circumstances had changed since that afternoon. *Joanne was in the room.*

Too much. Too fast. I explain that I thought she was teasing. We establish a signal, "Henry, I am serious" to avoid confusion.

I suggest we need to compromise as in, "OK, five minutes only. I'm tired of cuddling."

We go to bed without cuddling. But in the early morning hours we find each other again in the big bed.

* * *

This is a speed bump on the road to happiness but I have hit my head.

I get up early and go out. I feel bruised and want to sulk. I want to punish Cecilia by making myself scarce. But on reflection, I see it as a misunderstanding, which should be forgotten.

Later, I tell Cecilia it's perfectly normal to have misunderstandings and fights. In future we'll compromise.

"A lover is never your enemy," I say. "A lover never brings bad. Just say, stop that's bad and I'll stop."

It takes three hours of holding to get the energy between us flowing again.

After a day or so, the fight is forgotten.

* * *

Walking back to our room, Cecilia says she met an American missionary at the pool who speaks a local language. She's impressed.

I twig to her use of the word "impressed" and ask if she's impressed with me.

"Yes," she replies.

"Not just my money?"

She recoils, taking a few steps back. "No!"

* * *

We take the taxi to Sunday mass as the sun begins to set on Devao.

In the cab, Cecilia is wearing her public face, serious and stern. I can see how she'll look at 45. She'll look fine. Her father called her a "girl with a million faces." A few of them were pretty ugly but I ignored them for the beautiful ones. As we near the church, her face becomes devout, an earnest choir girl of 15.

I am tuned out but I am getting used to it.

The Cathedral is in the main square of this teeming city of over one million. It is large and wedge shaped, open on three sides. The services take place hourly all day long in two or three different languages. The people flow in and out like the tide. The pews are packed and there are hundreds standing at the back and in the aisles.

The sea of beautiful faces awes me.

"Stay here," I tell Cecilia. "I'm going to look around."

She pinches my wrist. "This is a mass," she says sternly. I stay put.

The service is simple, teaching these poor hard working people that helping those even less fortunate than themselves is the same as helping Christ.

The hymns are humble and sweet. There is a rush for the Eucharist with many long lines forming. Cecilia kneels and prays fervently.

I am sobbing. I don't know why. I have never seen such living religious fervor expressed in such a humble, unpretentious way.

My body is shaking in gratitude and relief. Gratitude for Cecilia's love which has delivered my weary soul out of 12 years of slavery in an Egypt of greed.

At the end, people are asked to bless those around them – smiles and handshakes are exchanged.

* * *

Rights Group seeks passage of law on 'desaparecidos': Human rights group have called on the government to pass a law that will punish perpetrators of involuntary disappearances or "desaparecidos." Data gathered by the families of victims of Involuntary Disappearance (FIND) showed that the number of desaparecidos has reached 1600 since the Marcos regime[ie. 15 a month]. (Philippine Star)

* * *

Monday we get up early and take our chaperon to the airport. Back at the hotel, Cecilia is poker faced as we walk to our room but I sense the excitement.

Joanne is as good as chaperons get but her absence seems to liberate Cecilia. She may be a Catholic virgin on the street, but between the sheets, she belongs to her tribe, the *Ilongo*: she is instinctive, ardent, natural.

I feel something mysterious and primal about her. I am making love to a thousands-year-old race of wayfarers who travel in catamarans under the stars.

After, we eat lunch in silence. I have a realization that in America, couples have to chat to feel connected. I tell Ceci it's good to be with a girl who doesn't talk unless she has something to say. I hate meaningless talk—it's tiring.

I read the newspaper. She reads the sports. This is what my former girlfriend and I did after a couple of years. What's the difference?

* * *

I exchange glances with the stunning hostess who stands outside the Chinese restaurant on the hotel premises. These glances are common here. They are a mutual acknowledgment: you're hot.

In America, women are on auction. The better looking they are, the more they think they're worth. They want to find the highest bid. Their message is: "You can't afford me." Here, the message is: "Love me. Love has no price."

I could find many excellent mates in the Philippines. But I was not going to put Cecilia on hold while I played the field. I got engaged to the first girl I fell in love with.

You go to a store for a hammer. Find a good one; you build a house. You don't waste your time examining other hammers.

* * *

Henry: Cecilia, how often are Filipinas disciplined by their husbands? Are they spanked weekly or monthly?
Ceci: That will not work.
Me: What will work?
Ceci: Carfare. (I can't understand her accent.)
Me: *Carfare?*
Ceci: Caress her!

* * *

In the pool, I talk with a handsome Englishman who sells English language training to Asian governments. He mentions he is married to a Malaysian woman and has three children.

After a while, I get a "look" from Cecilia some distance away.

"I'm being called," I say. "Is your wife the same?'

"Yes, Malay women all talk with their eyes."

Malay?

"Malaysia, Indonesia and Philippines; it's all the same stock. "
What's it like to be married to one?"

"You have to be very sensitive and perceptive to detect trouble brewing in advance because she won't spell it out."

Is the marriage good?

"We've been married 15 years and are very happy."

One more thing: Do you ever have conversations?

"Yes, but it takes time."

* * *

Something about Cecilia's last note stuck in my mind. The sentence: "I did not go before with a man if I just meet him for only a few days."

When did you go with a man before? I ask.

She said she was referring to her ex-boyfriend, an engineering student at MSU (Mindanao State University).

"Why did you break up with him?" I ask.

A cloud passes over her face and she gets all choked up.

She says she'll tell me later.

* * *

The phone rings. It's Andy and Joanne. Andy wants us back in three days (December 18). We had planned to stay another week but this seems like a fair compromise. I tell him we are in love and are going to get married.

In Maitum? he asks. Sure.

How did the engagement become marriage? The engagement

seemed like a trial period and I didn't want a trial. I have wasted enough time.

I now realize I have been stifled for the lack of a woman's love. At 48 I feel like my life has not begun. I have no real career, no relation to society.

A basic male instinct is to love a woman, have children and support them. It's what grounds a man, inspires him, and makes him part of the world. It's what's been missing from my life.

I had money but I didn't have a life. So I gambled. Now I want to use it to give Cecilia and our children a good life. She makes me want to pack a lunch pail and work in a factory.

When I see the love in Cecilia's face, the way she looks at me, I know with certainty she is a gift from God. I feel my life is finally beginning and it can't begin without this.

* * *

Tuesday Dec. 16.

Ten days in the Philippines. Wow. I am marrying the girl who just one week ago couldn't even look at me.

If it's folly, I would like to commit such folly more often.

Who could resist? Not getting married in the Philippines is like visiting Florida and not having an orange.

I got separated just three weeks after meeting another woman. Why shouldn't I get married in the same time span?

I look up from my writing pad and catch Ceci looking at me. She is taking such pleasure in me doing my thing. Her expression is full of love. Just like feminists to think a man needs an intellectual companion and not love.

* * *

I return to the room to find Cecilia sitting on the bed writing a letter. The atmosphere is funereal.

She is very upset. I can't imagine why. I beg her to tell me what's wrong but she won't. This is a long letter. I ask her to let me read the beginning.

"You wait."

What can it mean? She can't come to Canada? Her face is solemn.

I am pacing up and down. I assure her that things couldn't be so bad. I'll make them better. Just tell me. She ignores me.

After about a half-hour, she gives the letter to me. She takes the Gideon Bible and goes out onto the balcony.

Henry,

You said you are my boyfriend so I do hope you can understand if what I want to say but I will just write it 'coz if ever I don't want to remember this nightmare anymore. I know it's fair enough to tell you this. It always bothers me. My conscience I know it was not my fault. I don't know where I begin...You're asking me if what's the reason why my ex boyfriend and I broke up. It was really a nightmare. Tell me is it a fault to help him, to take care of him when he's sick (maybe my fault) he raped me you know. & my mama knows about it.& my mother once decided that the guy & I will get married & the guy agreed but I was the one who refused (But my papa don't know all about it.) I'm very open with my mama 'coz I know she can understand me. See, she's also a woman. (that was last year month of Nov.) If I'm not a Christian & don't have faith in God, all I think that time is I want to commit suicide. I wanna die. Everyday seeing him in the university was hell. the reason why I didn't used to stay in one place last yr. 2nd sem. & affected my studies a lot. &it coincides that my father got sick in February & I have the reason to go home every weekends.& I gave that reason to stop 'coz that time I was really depressed & hate the world. I want to be alone all the time but pretending ok in front of my friends.

There was only one person I depend on except my mother, a sailor (pen pal) whom I treat as a trusted friend. He cheer me up, give me courage & let me know that God is always there. Remember the letter you saw addressed in France. He's the one, a Filipino, fresh graduate from the Phil Merchant Marine Academy & he said he's still there (courting me) & wants me to be his wife after his ten months of contract 'coz he said no matter what happened 'coz what he likes in me is the inner personality. About my ex-boyfriend he is still hoping that we'll be back one of these days, he even sent me a message in Maitum. Maybe to see that I will be with him again. No way. Can you imagine what hap-

*pened. It was really a nightmare & always bothers me. I'm always pray-
ing that God will give me the man who's not that kind of monster.*

In the Philippines, rape is punishable by death or life in prison.

Cecilia is in steel coil mode. I carry her to the bed. Clutching the
Gideon Bible to her chest, she is begging God for help in her native
Tagalog language. Eventually I pry the Bible away from her and try to
focus her mind on the future. Don't worry about forgiving your ex-
boy friend. Forget him. You are still a virgin until you give yourself to
a man. You're still a virgin to me.

I have so much experience calming women in various stages of
hysteria that I do this almost in automatic pilot. We make love without intercourse and fall asleep in each other's arms.

Later I ask her if she had confessed the rape to her parish priest.
She had and he had absolved her. The rape and its aftermath explain
the preternaturally old expression on her young face, what I call her
"police woman" look. But sexually, she exhibits no fears or inhibi-
tions as a result of her trauma. Quite the opposite.

* * *

Next morning Cecilia seems to be relieved and cheerful. She is
doing her laundry by hand and offers to do mine.

I'm sitting on the balcony smoking a cigarillo. One week in the
Philippines. I've had too much sex. It's starting to feel like a duty. I
need a break.

I have the wisdom to know what I want and accept it gratefully. But
this is not all of me. I need to sit and smoke and reflect. She appears
at the door. I tell her to stop bothering me. We need to spend time
apart to enjoy being together. She doesn't like my smoking.

Do you want to be a good wife? I ask her.

Yes.

Permit me my sins. I will permit yours. Lets give each other lots of
room.

* * *

We're sitting side by side in a travel agent's office in a mall surrounded by beautiful women. This is my first inkling of how hard it
will be to get Cecilia back to Canada. There is two months of red tape
just to get a Philippine passport.

"Just promise me one thing," I ask Cecilia.

"What?"

"You'll talk to me."

"I weel" (without hesitation)

* * *

At supper I tell her: "You chose me by loving me. I don't care if
you ever talk."

She seems relieved. After supper, I go to the washroom. Don't talk
to any men, I kid her.

When I return, she says Tom Cruise tried to pick her up.

He's better looking than me. But I am a better man than Tom
Cruise. And you are a better woman than Nicole Kidman. I would
choose you over any Hollywood starlets.

Cecilia: " Why?"

"Because they are very demanding. Their love is conditional on
meeting *their* standards. I want to be myself. I'll do what I want. I
want to be loved for myself."

Cecilia: "It's very hard to wear a mask."

* * *

Dialogue in bed in the dark:

Cecilia: What are you doing?

Me: I am looking for something.

Cecilia: You will not find it there.

Me: I have already found it.

Cecilia: What is it?

Me: My lost youth.

* * *

At breakfast, I tell Cecilia that she can serve herself this morning. My serving her was a gesture, not a way of life. And this morning I will get the front section of the newspaper first, and she'll have to wait to read the sports.

I love you but I also love me. Otherwise there won't be me for you. She returns to the room first. I linger in the lobby. I want to miss her.

I reflect on my past. Generalization: Women in America are so busy trying to be independent of men, they miss ever having a man.

My ex. A feminist. Why didn't she just give herself to me? Surrender? Trust? Like Cecilia? Maybe then I would have fallen in love with her too.

There was a beautiful piece of land by the river. I considered building a house. I didn't. Unconsciously I knew better.

* * *

My sexual response is not what it should be.

Is it satiation? No. It's emotional. Cecilia is too quiet. I explain the problem to her. I need her to say, "I love you," "I belong to you," if she feels that. She learns quickly and, ironically, is quite verbal in the act.

The next morning, our last in Davao, we consummate our love.

"I love you, I love this," she says afterward.

We rush through breakfast and taxi to the airport. In the waiting room, a couple of large ruddy looking European males gobble Cecilia up with their eyes.

We take the Mindanao Express Beechcraft to General Santos Airport. There, a mob of taxi drivers and porters clamor for our business.

Cecilia needs to go 20 km to pick up her clothes at the boarding house where her Aunt Veronica lives near the asparagus packing plant.

No sooner do we get to Veronica's tiny room with two beds, when Veronica's roommate Rosana, challenges me.

"Cecilia is too young for you."

"You are jealous," I reply.

"No I'm just being blunt."

'What's the right age?"

"24-25" (her age)

"What is the difference between Cecilia and a 24-25-year-old?"

"Cecilia is not broadminded."

"You don't know her. She is a woman, not a child. I know her better than you."

I am right. In the cab, Cecilia explains that the roommate knew her only two days. We stop at the asparagus plant where Veronica has taken more of Cecilia's clothes. A measure of the security is that after much back-and-forth on the walkie-talkie, the guard won't let her get her clothes.

Back on the road, Cecilia explains that she is treated like the baby by her extended family. They want her to marry Gerry, the Filipino merchant sailor. Cecilia has corresponded with Gerry for three years but they have never met.

She gives me one of his letters. He seems like a good man. Says he's earning tons of money and wants to start a business in Manila. He is preparing Cecilia to be his wife, and instructs her to be "disciplined" and "courteous."

We take a taxi to the mall where we buy a mattress, a fan, a tablecloth and other kitchen stuff. Then it's to the van terminal for the two-hour ride to Maitum.

Andy and Mely are very happy to see their daughter.

As we unload the mattress, I joke that, like the Princess in the story, I must sleep on a mattress. They will have it after their daughter leaves. But Andy ignores me. I must remember that he is a proud man.

Cecilia has been aloof. Her face assumed a daughterly profile as we approached Maitum. I have my usual attack of insecurity. "Can you say anything to reassure me?" I ask her.

"I love you," she says.

Later I cajole her into lying with me on her new mattress. Her face is suffused with love. "I meese you," she whispers.

This is the heady stuff with which I must now be content.

Chapter Three

※

Trying to Get Married

We go to see if the priest will marry us.

Entering the manse, I glimpse a winsome figure in a white frock sweeping the church floor. I strain to see her face. The irony is not lost on me. There is a large Christmas tree in the priests' quarters. On the wall is a large poster of a dog: "Happiness is a warm puppy."

Father Joseph is about 35. He questions me about my religion and my previous marriage. I say I believe in the teachings of Christ but I can see he is skeptical. Finally he says he can't marry us without my divorce papers. If only I had brought them!

Then it's off to see the town registrar. There the problem is I need a "letter of legal capacity" from the Canadian Embassy in Manila. This states that I am single. Much time is spent trying to navigate around all this red tape without avail. So much for impetuous love.

In the evening Cecilia comes up to her room where I am lying on her comfortable mattress. "Embassy permission is necessary for us to marry," she says. "Papa will not let me come to Canada unless I am married. So you had better get permission."

I resent her tone of voice. "Never speak to me in a harsh tone like that. The easy part was in Davao. That's over now. We must not let circumstances undermine our love."

We lie together. "We must keep our connection strong even though we are in your father's house. I am a lover. Love is like breathing. I can't stop breathing."

We hug and caress. This week in Maitum might be bearable after all.

"I can't be near you and never see that tender expression on your face. The love in your eyes."

I tell her that the letters she had shown me from Gerry and other pen pals had made me feel insecure, like one of a crowd.

She says she'd never tell me if she were insecure.

"But I could read it in your eyes."

She starts to sing a song by a group called "Firehouse."

You know you're everything to me.
And I could never see
The two of us apart
And you know I'd give myself to you
And no matter what you do
I promise you my heart.
(Refrain)
I will build my world around you/ I just can't live without you
And I want you to know
I need you like I never needed anyone before.
(Chorus)
I live my life for you.
I wanna be by your side.
In everything you do.
&if there's only one thing
You can believe is true.
I live my life for you.

The word junkie is on cloud nine.

Later I ask Andy if Cecilia can sleep beside me on her mattress at night. No sex.

"Not until you are married," he says. "It is our tradition."

On our way to a prayer meeting, I relay this conversation to Cecilia: "I wanted to save you another night on the hard floor."

"I am used to it," she says.

At the prayer meeting, an older gentleman asks me if I am Catholic.

"No, Jewish. The people who brought you Jesus Christ."

Do you believe in Christ?

"Certainly do."

Do you believe Christ is God?

I consider this for a moment. "Yes I do."

The man is satisfied and turns away.

"And so are you," I say, under my breath.

* * *

Returning to the house, after the prayer meeting, Andy says Cecilia must get married before she can leave. "It's our tradition, our custom." he says.

"And you must also take a week-long seminar from Father Joseph on Catholic marriage."

Well that's the limit. "I have a tradition too; I am not a Catholic. She can be. I'm not going to any seminar."

Andy quickly concedes the point. We'll get married in a Pentecostal church.

Looking at Cecilia's photo album, I ask to see a picture of her ex-boyfriend.

She takes it out of her wallet and gives it to me. I am surprised she carries it in her wallet and say so. I won't give it back, and she accepts this without a word. I don't think she needs any connection with him.

* * *

I am getting frustrated with her reserve at home. Every time I kiss her, she looks right and left guiltily. The kisses have to be short and soundless. Hugs are furtive.

"I must respect my parents," she keeps saying.

She wants me to extend my stay beyond Christmas Day, but I don't see the point. The debate rages in my mind: "Look you had everything in Davao, now you have something else. She loves you. But she loves her parents too. Be content with memories. "

This doesn't work. I start spending time by myself away from the house. They know something is wrong. Eventually Andy finds me sitting in the park. I tell him I am very frustrated. I am ready to marry his daughter but she won't let me hold or kiss her in the house.

We strike a deal: she can lie with me day and night in her bed. No sex.

Andy says: "I trust you. But I have many friends here. I must be careful. I go in the street and they see me. What are they thinking?"

And the house is owned by the church. They live rent-free.

* * *

Later, hugging. Her expression: love.
Henry: "Who taught you to love?"
Cecilia: "You did!"
Henry: "I didn't teach you to love. Your parents did."

* * *

Mely isn't around very much and when she is, after 11 hours of work, she looks dazed with exhaustion.

I tell Andy and Mely that Cecilia and I will help them so Mely doesn't have to work so hard. Next week, we'll go to General Santos and open a bank account so I can wire money in the future. About $1200 US would provide a comfortable cushion for a year.

Andy says he trusts me like a son. I say I love him like a father. He is a loving father to Cecilia, a good decent man.

Andy is a handyman who can fix anything from motorcycles to radios to typewriters. He also does carpentry, masonry and metalwork. He was born in the northern part of the Philippines and fought with the U.S.-backed guerillas against the Japanese during World War Two.

After the war, he worked and studied in Manila before coming to Mindanao to work in a lumber camp. He supported his mother and many siblings for years. Many people, even the natives in the mountains, like him. He can go to them.

He is afraid the Moslem rebels will kidnap me, and urges me not to flash bills.

* * *

Sunday Dec. 21, 1997

Last night is the first night we share a bed in her father's house. Cecilia starts by giving me the distant treatment. A few perfunctory kisses. Good night. No cuddling. Her parents are behind the thin walls.

"I am leaving Monday," I say.

"No," she whispers.

She is a little more available but forcibly restrains my hand.

At 3.30 a.m. A dog's extended and insistent barking awakens me.

At 4.30 a.m. the church's PR system next door starts blaring Christmas Carols to summon parishioners. "*We wish you a merry Christmas, we wish you a merry Christmas*," blares into my weary soul. It can be heard for miles.

How do non-Catholics tolerate this intrusion? I demand.

"Tradeeshon."

Well then, I will wake Father Joseph at 4.30 a.m. on Chanukah. My tradition.

I tell Cecilia I will not tolerate any more games around cuddling. I have made a big bet on our love and when she repels me, I feel like I have made the wrong bet. I don't like that feeling.

Do you love me?

Yes.

No more games, OK?

She consents.

As Cecilia leaves for church, I mutter, "Have something to eat. The crackers they serve aren't very filling."

* * *

Sunday night I invite the family and Joanne to a restaurant. I ask Joanne to help me find one that is open. I need a break from Cecilia so we slip away unnoticed. We decide on the restaurant owned by the Mayor and Joanne decides to wait for us there. They put chicken on the BBQ for us.

I return to the house to learn that Cecilia had followed us. This is a little troubling since it is very dark. But I assume that she will either find Joanne or return to the house.

When we arrive at the restaurant, Cecilia is not there. She knew we were going out to eat. I could not believe she would be absent unless something was wrong.

I take charge. I send Andy and Mely back to the house to wait for her there. Joanne stays at the restaurant to bring the food when it is ready. Meanwhile I search the streets of the darkened village.

I peer at the shadowy figures of young women but none turn out to be Cecilia. Could she have been kidnapped? Will I, the rich American, be asked for ransom? I imagine her at that moment with her tormentors. I make the rounds of other restaurants. No one has seen Cecilia. "Calbo" I hear people say as I go by ("bald man"). I ask in the market. I crisscross the ghostly village in a frenzy. No sign of her.

Things were going so well. Why did I leave her behind? I go over the moment we left without her and wish I could have it back again. Then, some youths call out from a bench under a tree. "Hey Joe! (all white men are GI Joes) Cecilia went home."

I thank them, and rush to the house.

I find Cecilia there looking shaken. She had been "giving advices" to a distraught friend. I find this incomprehensible.

"Did your father scold you?" She ignores me.

"I just wanted a little space," I say. "Do you have to follow me like a little puppy?"

Soon Joanne arrives with the food. She also provides the distraction as I tease her about disappointing her pen pals by becoming a nun.

After supper Cecilia wants to go out with Joanne.

After what you have put us through tonight, do you have to go out?

"I need some space, some time alone with Joanne." This seems like revenge.

She promises to be back in a half-hour. Mely goes with them. I am alone with Andy. Cecilia's behavior is setting off alarms. It feels like adolescent rebellion. I am supposed to sign the marriage contract tomorrow and I am worried. My conversation with Andy doesn't help.

He says his daughter is spoiled, immature. "I gave her everything. Clothes. Schooling."

The half-hour stretches into an hour and Cecilia isn't back. She promised. I feel slighted. The signing of the marriage contract looms large as the minutes tick by.

"You know Andy, I am uneasy about marrying Cecilia now. She said she'd be back in a half-hour. Look at the time. She is dishonoring me."

Andy agrees.

"Maybe it's best that Cecilia and I don't get married right away," I say.

"I am afraid of what people will think if Cecilia goes to Canada and is not married," Andy responds.

"Just tell them she is living with other girls, not with me. You don't have to be so candid."

Andy ponders this. I continue: "We don't want a divorce. There is no divorce in the Philippines."

Andy agrees that marriage is sacred for his people; divorce would be unthinkable.

"Let's not rush. I am afraid that Cecilia is going to have a rebellious period and it will fall on my head. We'll stay engaged."

Andy and I shake on it.

Cecilia and Mely come in. They walked Joanne home. I realize immediately that I am overreacting. I don't mention the engagement idea but she senses something in the air.

Later I mention it in bed. I am worried about her rebelling against me. Cecilia pens another letter:

I'm troubled, you know. Just like you I'm only human being & don't expect too much from me. When you said to me that it's better to get engaged first I'm very much willing to know each other first 'coz to us that's really the way. Long courtships to get to know each other, so nothing to regret & like you I don't want a fight 'coz I'm tired of it. I mean I don't fight my ex-boyfriend but he's a very jealous guy. & I also sacrificed a lot for him—opportunities (offers) especially. He always confront me – who's this guy, who's that guy...where are you this day and that time. I really sacrificed a lot for him and I adjust. We always broke-up, maybe 20 times.

Although it's a bad experience I'm still grateful that I had been given a chance to meet trials in order get matured -college life gave me a lot of lessons. But I know in some ways I'm still acting as a girl. As I said there's a right time for everything. All I need is a man who will understand me. Remember I'm only 18. Maybe you're right better to be engaged first -It's better not to sign the contract first. So that the registrar will not wait for the papers to arrive & to disturb them. You know I don't want to be the talk of the town after this.

We could sign the contract if both of us are really sure to get married, ok? What if I'm not the kind of lady you are looking for? You know what I'm bothered for your impatientness & you always change your mind. Maybe you're expecting too high from me & that's I'm worried about — -Like you I don't want a fight so that's the reason I don't say words when you're talking & don't want to begin or have the fight (quarrel).

After I read this letter, we have the closest thing to a normal conversation I have had with her. She tells me that the reason she was missing at supper was that she ran into a "desperate suitor", a former neighbor who was courting her and was threatening to commit suicide over her impending marriage. She had met him and his friend by accident and had to talk to them.

I apologize for underestimating her and she forgives me. She says her dad doesn't know her anymore since she spent two years away at college. He thinks she's a spoiled kid. He doesn't know about the rape, or about the desperate suitor.

She says we are the talk of the town. There are rumors that our visits to Dr. Juni were because Cecilia is already pregnant. She says she will have to "roam around town" to learn what people are saying.

I ask her how she can be *afraid* to speak to me. She says it's because of her experience with her ex boyfriend.

* * *

Monday Dec. 22, 1997

A company, "Byantel", provides a telephone link via microwave between Maitum and the outside world. You go to their office and, after a wait, they connect you on one of their two lines.

After many attempts, I finally get through to a real person at the

Canadian Embassy. I do need the certificate of legal capacity and I have to go to the embassy in Manila to get it. I need to prove I am single.

I phone my friend, Todd, who has my house key and ask him to fax my divorce certificate to the embassy. He seems cooperative but aloof. I learn later that Cheryl was incensed by my plans, and was opposed to his helping me. He literally had to back into a closet with the phone to get some space. He did send the fax in spite of her opposition.

The Mayor's restaurant is across the street. After the phone calls, I go there for a drink. The Mayor's wife brazenly asks me if I am sleeping with Cecilia. I tell her it 's none of her business but we aren't. Filipinos are the nosiest people on earth.

I sign my part of the marriage contract at the town registrar's office. I am told this will come into effect when the Certificate of Legal Capacity arrives.

Cecilia is taciturn, distant, driving me crazy. The roosters are crowing, the dogs are barking. The heat and stares are getting to me. As I make my rounds, trying to get married, I pass a bullfrog flattened on the road. Is this me?

Later, Andy confronts me. The registrar told him the contract is useless.

Why? You must have the certificate of legal capacity. *I know that.*

I have to protect my daughter. *Look I'll get it. I'm doing everything in my power. Can't you see that?*

After I return, with news of solid progress, Cecilia is more upbeat. Clearly, she wants certainty; she wants marriage. I am rewarded with French kisses.

* * *

Andy, Cecilia and I walk to the van. We are going to General Santos to open the bank account and extend my visit. Andy wants me to keep my hand on my wallet.

"Leave me alone," I say. "You paranoids are driving me crazy."

Cecilia starts making "crazy" hand signs at my head.

When we get to the van, Andy apologizes for his earlier outburst. "I think of you as a son," he says.

In General Santos, Philippine Airways extends my return ticket for one week without charge. The visa extension costs $25. The government official tells me "Filipinos are very loving people." He looks at Cecilia and says she will make a good "human blanket" on those cold winter nights in Canada.

Next stop is the Philippines National Bank where I open an account in Cecilia and her father's name depositing what Andy earns in a month. I get the address for wiring funds. The bank has closed by the time the paper work is done and we are regurgitated into the sunshine through a back door.

Neither Cecilia nor Andy says a word about my gesture. "I've never seen such ungrateful people in my life," I say to no one in particular.

"You wait," Cecilia says.

"I'm sorry but we have a tradition in Canada that when someone does something for you, you say 'thanks.'"

Andy turns and gives me a heartfelt, "thanks."

"You're welcome," I reply, equally gracious and grateful.

We take a tricycle to a busy department store where we buy a cooler to serve as a refrigerator. I buy some underwear. Cecilia takes the cue to pick out some bras and panties that I pay for. Pointedly, she doesn't thank me.

* * *

We share a taxi back to Maitum. On the way, night descends on the tropics and there is a ferocious downpour. In the driving rain, we pass an ox stoically standing alone, and a flock of 200 ducks waddling toward us with some urgency.

We arrive safely and I give the driver a big tip. A little later I glimpse the arrival of Cecilia's 84-year old grandmother, three aunts and cousin Gilbert, age 9. The expression on Grandma's face is sneaky, like she is crashing an event. They have come for the wedding but we were supposed to invite them first.

When we arrived, Cecilia was affectionate. "Thanks for everything." she said.

But later, alone in her room, she breaks free when I try to embrace her: "We must respect my grandmother."

I have a visceral reaction. I am doing everything to make her my wife yet I cannot even depend on her affection when I want it. I am furious.

I sit in the backyard smoking a cigarillo and fuming. I'm mad enough to leave town. I decide to go for a walk. As I leave, Cecilia introduces me to two young guys sitting on a bench outside in the dark.

"Henry, these are my friends Roland and Arthur," she says.

"Nice to meet you," I say to the shadowy figures, "Excuse me, I'm going for a walk."

"Nice to meet you," they say, without conviction.

It occurs to me that these two might be the "desperate suitor" and his friend.

But I am not sure, and I am angry with Cecilia. I feel like a rebuffed teenager and it's humiliating. Voices call out "Joe" or "Calbo" as I pass plotting revenge. I will spend the next five days avoiding her. I will not touch her or attempt to kiss her.

Returning, the two guys are still sitting there.

At supper, Cecilia confirms that they are the "desperate suitor" and his friend. For the second night running, they are ruining our supper. Andy will not invite them in because he doesn't like them.

We need their bench so I get it hoping they will get the message. But they don't. They squat in the yard in the dark, like a couple of toms. The tobacco has made me a bit queasy.

"Cecilia is engaged to be married. Leave her alone," I tell them. "Maitum is full of beautiful women."

The guys' friend: "We have not come to quarrel. We want to settle things."

But before I can ask what exactly they have to settle, Cecilia intervenes between us, as if we were going to exchange blows. She pushes me inside. But not before I threaten to call the police. They slink away in the dark.

Inside Cecilia is sitting on the stairs crying. I don't know why.

I sit on a higher step watching her sob. My sister was right. This is what I get for robbing the cradle. My dream girl: crying like a baby.

At the same time, she needs my protection. I retreat to her room. Eventually she joins me on her bed for comfort.

Why are you crying? I ask. Her father had smacked her across the head.

I lay it out for her. You can't try to be friends with Roland. You're just confusing him.

I am tired of you "respecting your grandma", "respecting your father" but not respecting me. I am going to be your husband. *I must be your first priority.* You must respect me before your father and your grandmother. When I want you, you must be there. I am there when you want me.

She seems to understand this, and agrees.

The house is full of snoring sounds. Grandma's asthma makes her sound like an ox. Rats crash across the roof like subway trains. Lizards make clucking sounds. Firecrackers explode like bombs. The Backstreet Boys' song, "*As Long As You love Me*" echoes from the town gymnasium where the basketball game is at half time. In a few hours the church will start broadcasting kitschy Christmas carols. Dogs bark.

Cecilia is asleep in my arms. I am calm again, happy.

* * *

Three items from a Philippines radio news broadcast. Dec. 22 1997.

Philippine banana workers have won a millions dollar settlement against the chemical arms of Shell Oil and Occidental Petroleum. They have become impotent from pesticides banned in America in 1970 but sold in the Third World until the 1990's.

Illegal logging and deforestation has destroyed a valuable watershed 100 miles north of Davao.

Most rebel groups get their arms from raiding outposts of the Philippine army, and not from outside sources.

* * *

Cecilia is having her period so I go swimming with Gilbert. Gilbert found my missing watch under my bed and I rewarded him with 10 pesos. He is a doughty self-sufficient child, so happy to be swimming he doesn't require any attention whatever.

After two hours at the beach, Gilbert and I start walking back to town. To pass the time I teach him to count to ten in English. He hardly speaks any English.

He learns quickly. I teach him to count from ten to twenty.

A bright child, he soon masters this.

I have a profound sense of satisfaction. This is real. Teaching.

Why can't I devote myself to teaching poor motherless children like Gilbert, so beautiful, loyal and loving instead of playing money games squandering what would be an unthinkable fortune for these people?

How poor and depraved I am in my wealth. My inner poverty is why no amount of money is ever "enough".

A thong comes out of my beach slipper. I am searching the ground for something to push it into place with. I see a stick. Without my saying a word, Gilbert hands it to me.

How rich these people are in their poverty. They have a love, which comes from constantly observing their beloved and anticipating their needs. It comes from taking from their own mouths to feed their loved ones.

My country is rich but we are poor in what counts, love. That's why we are so fat, fearful and stingy.

We worship Gold. Nothing has changed since Moses.

Gilbert and I walk along the road bordered by rice paddies and coconut trees. Hymns emanate from a revival meeting.

"21-22-23-24-25-26-27-28-29-30" Gilbert continues.

"Who taught you to count to 30?" I demand.

"School," Gilbert says. "I can count to 1000."

Chapter Four

Christmas in Maitum

I give Andy 1000 pesos to buy a pig to roast in the Filipino Christmas tradition.

Instead, he buys pork pieces because pigs are too expensive. This turns out for the better. The pig at the wealthy neighbor's Christmas party is a big disappointment, mostly fat and gristle.

As the pig, so the party. The only interesting thing for me is a conversation with Ed, Cecilia's handsome friend and fellow student at MSU. He asks me why I came to the Philippines in search of a woman.

I tell him that many women in America are self centered, neurotic, ambitious and masculine. The nice ones find me too old. He agrees that Philippine women are "very loving" and "submissive." He seems to take that for granted, and instead, finds independent women more alluring.

Ed's use of the word "submissive" rings a bell.

I had told myself that I wanted a "traditional" woman. I did not dare to consider the word "submissive." But damn it! That's exactly what I want!

After talking to Ed, I decide to go back to the house. I ask Cecilia to come home and make a cup of coffee for me.

"Get it yourself, you fucking asshole," I can almost hear her American sisters.

I leave. Five minutes later I hear Cecilia downstairs making a cup of coffee.

She brings me the coffee. I put it aside and pull her down on the bed.

"Are you a submissive woman?" I ask her.

"What does submissive mean?" she asks.

It means you obey your husband.

"I obey you because I love you," she says.

"And I'll never do anything to weaken your love," I vow.

* * *

Many educated women in America have no desire to please men. The very idea seems absurd to them. They've had such a raw deal for so many centuries, men should please *them!* They are our latest persecuted minority.

The persecution women have experienced is shameful. While men were dying by the millions to defend the country in two world wars, some women were forced to work in hospitals and factories. While men for centuries have performed hard labor in mines and forests to support their families, women were forced to nurture their own children!

Yes. An American woman will try to please a man. *If she wants something.* It's called trade: you please me; I'll please you.

In the next few days I experience the joys American men don't even know they've lost. Without being asked, Cecilia does my laundry by hand, folds my clothes, organizes my suitcase, cuts my finger and toenails (with selfish motive.)

She shaves off all my hair. (I have male pattern baldness.) She says I'll look younger if I get rid of the gray. And I do.

She pulls out the gray from my eyebrows. Only we can't find a position from which she can wield the tweezers. Finally I settle my head (face up) between her bare young thighs. (She is wearing shorts.)

This is bliss. The energy between a beautiful young woman's thighs is amazing. The Garden of Eden. When the job is over, it feels like the Fall of Man.

* * *

At breakfast, I ask for eggs.

"Why? You already have two," Cecilia says

Cecilia loves to tease me. She pinches my chin and accuses me of being fat.

Luckily she has a bit of flab under her chin, a racial characteristic. I reply by pinching that and saying, *"He who is without chin should cast the first stone."*

Another time I tell her, "I want you to keep your identity when you come to Canada. I am getting rid of the washing machine."

She threatens to swat me.

My anxiety dissipates the more time I spend with her. She is so loving, smart and funny.

On a rainy afternoon, she entertains me by making funny faces. She does an excellent platypus. Then, using a cigarette as a prop, she does the faces of everyone in a café: the waitress, the businessman, the actress. Her face is a phenomenon. One time when I awake her from a deep sleep, I disturb an angry demon. She makes a face that is not of this world. I beat a hasty retreat.

* * *

Gilbert is crying because they took his ten pesos to buy ice for the cooler. He is soon reimbursed. Money is a preoccupation for Cecilia's grandmother and aunts. Cecilia's grandmother complains incessantly about how two of her daughters married Germans and wrote off the family.

She complains how Eleanor, one of the three aunts that came, took her pension money and now she can't buy medicine for her asthma. A split develops. Eleanor and the other aunts leave early. Gilbert refuses to leave and stays with his grandma.

"I'm sick of hearing about money," Cecilia says. "This is why we live in Maitum and they live in General Santos."

Eleanor didn't leave before relieving the good-natured Cecilia of 200 pesos. I scold Cecilia. "I can't support your whole family."

On departure, Eleanor tries to hit up Cecilia again. She is all smiles and solicitude for her niece but nothing doing this time.

"Eleanor is a bloodsucker," Andy says later.

* * *

Supper, Christmas Day 1997

"I must be honest with you," suddenly Andy is saying. "I am an honest man. It's a long story. I'll tell you after supper."

"No," Cecilia says. "I'll tell him."

Please Andy, you tell me. I'll get old waiting for Cecilia to talk.

While they are deciding who will tell, I guess it. Cecilia is adopted.

Mely had two babies die in infancy. Andy prayed to God. "Please give me any kind of child. I will take care of her." Then he went to see the priest, Father Melo. Two years passed before his prayers were answered.

Cecilia was brought to his home at age three days in swaddling clothes by a nurse. Father Melo had arranged it and even gave Cecilia her name.

Cecilia' s birth mother had two other children and no means of support. She was married but not to Cecilia's father who paid the hospital bill.

Cecilia has known she was adopted since the age of five. There were schoolyard rumors that she was a "bamboo child" (a reference to Moses in the reeds). She rummaged through the house until she found the adoption papers and confronted her parents with them.

A few days later, I ask her if it made her feel insecure.

"Sometimes," she says with her usual verbosity.

* * *

Sunday Dec. 28, 1997

I dream of wanting to throw my ex-girlfriend out of my house but she won't leave.

We have a big fight. I awake and realize that she moved out a year ago. I feel immense relief.

The people of Maitum don't stare at me any more. The novelty has worn off. The feeling is mutual. It's time to move on. I have had enough of the beach. Cecilia and I are coasting.

I desperately need some space. I tell Cecilia that she is 50% of my life; the other 50% needs my attention. Naturally she is sullen about my departure, and selfish man, I find it unsettling. I want her to express what I feel, gratitude for what we have been given, and relief at getting a break from it all.

"The future is knocking and demanding that we make it happen," I say. "Let's march, not sulk."

Andy agrees to let us spend our last night at a hotel in General Santos. "I will not forget you," he says, as we part.

On the way, I have a minor revelation. I have more in common with Cecilia and her family than I think. Poverty. My grandparents were as poor as Cecilia's parents. They were Polish Jews who lived in a room and each month pleaded with the landlord for more time to pay the rent. Poverty made my parents and they made me. It is a teacher of universal values.

In the van, Cecilia asks me "Ayos lang?" In Tagalog, it means "Are you alright?"

Maybe she thinks I should be miserable, but love is like food. You can't eat all the time. You get sick of it.

We take a room with a jacuzzi in The Royal, the best hotel in General Santos.

My fantasy meter should be going wild. I am alone with the beautiful willing woman I love.

But somehow I feel impassive. We bathe together, we make love. Something is not what it should be. I am turned on by love. Sex doesn't do it for me anymore. And Cecilia is in a funk and even more aloof than usual.

Rather than empathize with her, as I should have, I am annoyed. "Can't you talk to me? Is that asking so much?" I say. She flicks channels on the TV, ignoring me.

I pretend to go to sleep without even saying goodnight. Finally she turns off the light without saying anything. A few minutes pass in the dark. I want to hear her voice. I reach over, silently strip her and make love to her. It works.

"I love you," she says in the throes of passion. "I love you sweetheart. I need you. I'm crazy about you."

Her voice.

* * *

I had no right to reproach her that last night. I regret my behavior.

Why can't I relate to her *actions* instead of her words? She *acted* like we were an old married couple. She farted and laughed about it. "Carbon dioxide," she called it.

When I was taking a bath, she came in looking uncomfortable. *How intimate it would be if she peed in my presence.*

But before I could introduce the idea, she was already urinating and giggling.

We crossed the threshold. If Canadian Immigration demands evidence of our bond, this is better than any bundle of love letters. I'll send them a vial.

At the airport next morning, Cecilia is a lost puppy. I give her a *long* pep talk about how beautiful our future will be.

This cheers her up. She is nearly herself again. We embrace near the spot we met just 20 days ago.

"Ayos lang?" she says.

I nod.

And then she is gone.

It's 9 a.m. I wonder how long it will take until I miss her. At that moment she is the last person I want to see. For the record, I started to miss her at 5 p.m. the same day. About the time I'd be coming home from the factory.

* * *

On the plane to Manila, there is a young white guy and his beautiful Filipina bride sitting about ten rows behind me. I keep looking back at them, straining to see if they are … *talking.*

Collecting our luggage, I want to ask him, "Does she talk to you?" But I don't. The whole subject exhausts me.

I take a cab to Makati, a section of Manila that resembles any modern metropolitan city in the world. The taxi driver says, "Filipinos are poor but we have lots of children. They are our riches."

He is right. People are the most precious thing in the world. And Asia has more people than anyone: beautiful, hard working, loving people. Asia is rich.

We pass graffiti scrawled on a wall: "Your conscience is the voice of

God."

I check into a hotel that costs US$170 a night ($85 for the room and $85 for the marbled lobby.)

I get the "Letter of Legal Capacity" at the Canadian Embassy. If I mail it to Cecilia, we are married. I realize I can't do it. My behavior on the plane is the clue.

I write to Cecilia:

"Dearest Ceci, *I love you. I am not prepared to marry you <u>now</u> because you don't talk to me. Let us remain engaged. I need my wife to be a companion, someone who shares her experience, feelings, observations, at least to some degree. One who is curious about me. You say "I will". Then "We will" get married.*

At Manila Airport, I meet a handsome young Canadian who seems to have another of these yuppie merger marriages. He has been visiting his wife, an anthropologist evaluating an aid project in the Philippines. He also is in "the international development business" except his area of expertise is India.

I ask him if he competed with his wife.

"On the contrary," he says. "There is a synergy. Together we have the capacity of three anthropologists."

Businessmen always use the term "synergy" when they speak of a merger.

And, of course, modern couples refer to each other as "partners."

The long separations aren't a problem nor are children a priority. They certainly have passion but it isn't for each other.

Chapter Five

🔆

Back in Canada

I have changed. My love for Cecilia has brought God back into my life. I am finally out of the stock market. The pursuit of money is death. I rededicate my life to LOVE.

Work that I love. People that I love. Nothing else matters. Loving God and obeying Him. There is no other way. My energy levels are way up. I lose five pounds. I have no sexual desire. Only love turns me on. I concentrate on writing and looking after my game business.

Someone asked me if I had culture shock returning to Canada. It hits me when I visit a popular super bookstore one Saturday night in January. The people I see there –cosseted in their down-filled parkas and mutual funds—looked so bored, restless and lost.

Man has a choice: conversion or diversion. Clearly we have *not* converted. So what's left is self-seeking and a pursuit of distraction. T.S. Eliot called it a "wilderness of mirrors."

* * *

By their reactions, women over 40 find my actions extremely threatening.

My sister, 45, is divorced and has two sons age 17 and 20. She condemns my engagement on the basis of age and cultural difference. She is not interested in any information, not even in seeing Cecilia's picture.

She calls the engagement "outrageous, inappropriate, weird, socially unacceptable." I am "reckless, impulsive, always did what you wanted regardless...will live to regret it." I am "old enough to be her father. Just look at you, a middle aged Ph.D. marrying an 18-year-old girl. It will be a master-slave relationship."

She says I have "bought myself a young girl." Cecilia is "only after the money. She won't adapt to the culture. You'll have to go live in the Philippines."

Cecilia is a Catholic and my sister "doesn't like Catholics." When I accuse her of being a bigot, she amends this to "Catholics who persecuted Jews."

What's behind this venom? My sister resents that I don't find women her age sexually attractive. She is in love and engaged to marry a wonderful man my age.

"What do you care who I find attractive?" I ask. "You've got a man."

She has good friends who can't find men. They wouldn't want me, but nonetheless she is insulted for them.

When I suggest I want more children, her reaction is that I should be around to raise them. Not only is she determining whom I should love but also how long I have to live. "Your tentacles are all over my life," I tell her.

She also objects that my kids won't be Jewish. I counter that I've got a Jewish scion; I've done my bit for my people.

She resents she doesn't have "the same options."

"Do you think I like pot-bellied middle aged partners any more than you do?"

She later denied she'd want someone half her age. But if a handsome young stud swept her off her feet, I wonder how "socially inappropriate" *that* would be?

I wonder, how she can callously deny the legitimacy of my love, when she is in love herself? Doesn't she know how it feels? And I wonder where is her love for me? What did I do to her to unleash such hostility? I have been very supportive of her.

Cheryl, my best friend's wife, is a similar story. I offer to meet her again. But she doesn't want to be burdened by information. She talked to my sister and together they rehearsed my faults. Then she left a message on my answering machine saying I was immoral, no longer welcome at her home. "Don't phone and stay away from my kids," she said.

My escapades were coming at a time when there was stress in her marriage. Eventually Cheryl and Todd separated. Todd was calling his wife an "emotional bully." He resented the fact that she threatened to divorce him for sending the fax I requested.

At a Xmas party, she demanded he stop smoking a cigarette. When he refused, she dressed their three children and made a public spectacle of leaving.

* * *

My ex wife seems pretty cool. She just assumes Cecilia is doing this to come to this wonderful country.

Men, in general, see it as I do, a big but worthwhile gamble. They are fascinated to see how it turns out:

Peter (my old grad school buddy, happily married): "It's like a Twilight Zone episode. You're the man who got everything he wanted."

Danny (another friend from university days, happily married): " I think people these days are pretty tolerant. It's live and let live."

Barry (game store owner, maybe not so happily married): "You're lucky man. Relationships are all business now. Women are competing with us."

Ben (age 20, nephew): "If I were 48, I'd do it."

Evan (32, friend, bon vivant, living in Central America, by e-mail): " I'm delighted that you're in love. Of course it's impulsive and to say the least, unconventional. But most good things are."

Jim (36, longtime friend, ecstatically in love and engaged himself): His message is that he had found his soul mate, and I shouldn't settle for less just because I'm lonely. I explain my soul mate is God. I don't expect a woman to track my spiritual or intellectual trajectory. I just want to love and be loved.

Stan: (my brother, architect): He is skeptical that we could be so in love after only three weeks. You have nothing in common, he says. I reply that I'm not looking for a middle aged woman who protested the Vietnam war, got a Ph. D in English, invented games and smoked pot.

He wishes me well but advises that if I have any questions, "don't give her the benefit of the doubt." Anytime he's done that — with his ex wife or developers— he's regretted it.

And of course my best friend Todd, separated from Cheryl. He encourages me to pursue something that he regards as every man's fantasy. He wants to see how it unfolds.

A few common threads:

First, the more miserable people are, the more they hate what I'm doing. I'm definitely rattling their cages.

Second, it is amazing how much fear and distrust accompanies marriage on this continent. Love is a stranger; everything's business.

Third, even my best friends can't understand what Cecilia sees in me (other than money). This may explain why I had to go 8500 miles to find someone capable of loving me.

* * *

What a difference at the mall here compared to the Philippines. There, young women find me "hot". Here, they look right through me. I am dad, or worse

Downtown, a beautiful young colored girl meets my glance on a cold January day. I have to know if I needed to go 8500 miles. I make a remark about the cold.

"Yeah, it sucks," she says. She's 18, came from Eritrea with her folks when she was 12.

Are you single? I ask her.

No. she says.

Are you married?

Married? She is astonished. I'm too young. I have a boyfriend.

Obviously third world people here adopt Canadian standards. The teenagers are children.

Walking around a Canadian city in winter, it is hard to find any sexual energy.

I inquire about courses for Cecilia at a private college. The guidance officer, a redhead, about 30 is sexy, and seems to think I might have something to offer.

She looks me in the eye with an intent look. She gives me her card.

I feel I could ask her out.

I am practically a married man but it's nice to know I have options here too.

* * *

I am chatting with a psychiatrist I see once a month for another point of view.

I tell him that Cecilia's people have dignity.

"That's all they have," he says.

"They have soul. We don't. That's why you're so busy."

Our eyes fix for a long time.

I ask him if I'm a pervert for loving a woman so much younger than me.

No, he says. The majority of men would envy you.

I ask him if it'll work.

He says it stands a very good chance because Cecilia's expectations are so low, compared to an American girl her age.

Gee thanks. But it's encouraging anyway.

* * *

Cecilia is crying the first time she calls me.

She "meeses" me. But worse, she says the town has turned on her. Joanne has been talking and everyone knows she has been to bed with me without being married. Suitors are bothering her. They say she is not married yet. The "desperate suitor" has threatened to kidnap her.

Visions of the movie "Town Without Pity" flash through my mind. There, a German girl is lynched for having an affair with a GI after the war.

I tell Cecilia that she must go to live in Davao. I wire her money. She hasn't received my letter about postponing the marriage and, in her state, I don't have the heart to mention it.

The next time she calls, she isn't crying. Things have calmed down. She is living at home and spending a few days each week in General Santos to call me.

(There are no collect calls in Maitum.)

She has received my letter and is very hurt because I changed my mind.

"I'm just trying to do the right thing," I say.

She has been talking to Ed about the importance of conversation in marriage. She promises to "surprise" me when I next come.

She says Gerry has written and is coming to visit her. She is applying pressure.

Do you want to marry Gerry? I ask.

No.

Then don't mention him. Do you want to marry me?

Yes, she says definitely.

Would you love me if I were a poor man?

Yes.

For better or for worse?

"For better or for worse!"

OK I'll send you the letter of legal capacity.

Send it registered mail, she says.

I know she finagled me with talk of Gerry but I don't care. I want her.

* * *

Driving Josh home from school, I gripe about the traffic.

"According to Jean Paul Sartre, hell is other people. He must have been stuck in traffic."

What did Jean Paul Sartre do? Josh asks.

He was a philosopher. He invented existentialism.

What's that?

"A philosophy that was very important when I was young. It's the view that life has no purpose and people must make one up. "

You don't agree with that, do you? Josh says. He knows me.

* * *

I get a letter from another 18-year-old. Her name is Anne Marie and she is from Plan B, the only one to write me in Canada. She is cute but obviously much less mature than Cecilia. She is the youngest of eight children, six sisters and a brother.

She is a high school graduate but can't afford to go to college. She flatters me by writing, "more guys in other countries are sending me a letter but you're the one I'd like to respond to immediately."

I write her a polite note telling her I am engaged.

When Cecilia calls and taunts me that she has received a pen pal letter from a 26-year-old guy in the U.S., an MBA student at Harvard no less, I am able to respond in kind. Thanks Anna Marie.

Where's Gerry? I ask.

His ship has just passed through the Panama Canal.

You blackmailed me! I tease her.

"No," she protests. "I was just being open."

* * *

But suddenly Gerry's ship is nearing port and she's supposed to see him next day. She asks my permission. I give it. She's taking Ed along as a chaperon.

She is supposed to call the next day. She doesn't. I know there must be some explanation but I discover the meaning of "heartache" anyway.

I imagine that Gerry sweeps her off her feet. He takes the news of her engagement in stride and is completely supportive of her. She spends the day showing him the sights of General Santos. He is very handsome in his merchant marine uniform. She realizes she prefers a younger man. They elope together.

Another scenario. Her father wasn't feeling well. News reaches her that he has taken a turn for the worse. She goes to Maitum and can't phone. I am hoping Andy is on his deathbed, as preferable to Cecilia running off with Gerry.

Cecilia calls the next day. Gerry's ship didn't arrive after all. There was a nationwide protest strike against the price of gas. There was no transportation and she couldn't get to the telephone office.

The following day I receive this letter from her that I think will banish insecurity forever:

Evermine Henry,

Hi! How are you honey? (My darling "Kalbo," I'm just teasing you.) here's what you wished me to do, to write you & love sweetheart that's why I obey you. Are you doing fine in every way? I hope so…

So, here I am missing you a lot. How I miss seeing you around. Missing your kisses and holding me tight. & take note it's a cold night here so I need a human blanket! I miss you very badly. Terrible! & think I'm waiting for a long time. Each day is a sacrifice. How I wish also we could be together in attending the mass. I love you very much & I know you feel the same way too, aren't you?

When I went to MSU I had a talk with my ex boyfriend. Once and for all. But don't you worry you can trust me. It was just for the old time's sake. I have need to forgive him to have peace of mind. & I'm very thankful to God because of you. All I need is someone who can understand me. &that's what you are doing. Thanks for everything. For being good. For being there for me. For taking care and loving me. Hopin' that you will never ever change. You said I'm your first priority & you are also my first priority. I love you and I want to be with you for the rest of my life. Forever.

So long! I need to close because I'm sleepy and tired.

I love you, I miss you babe.

&take good care of yourself…

Hugs and kisses

Lots of love from

your baby,

Ceci

Chapter Six

Second Trip:
Marriage and Honeymoon

February, 1998.

I am leaving for the Philippines in a couple of hours to marry Cecilia. As I drive my son home from school, he asks some pointed questions.

"At this stage, didn't you feel exactly the same way about your last girlfriend?"

"Yes son. But Cecilia is different and so am I. This folly is completely different. Life is taking risks."

He had read this manuscript and wanted to know what I would do at times when I got tired of Cecilia.

"She'll have a job. Nobody can stand being together all the time."

At the Vancouver airport, Peter and I have our usual discussion. He believes that Lee Harvey Oswald killed Kennedy. And Tim McVeigh was responsible for Oklahoma City.

I scoff: "The information we get from the media is like an IV drip to a comatose patient."

Peter's father left him a comfy stock portfolio that seems to dictate his politics. Plus he has a government job. You'd think money would make us free, but instead it holds us prisoner. Look at me. I am hoping for war in the Persian Gulf so I can sell my oil drilling stocks. Ironically I never cared about money until I had some. Then it took over my identity.

Waiting for the plane, I talk to Mark, an American who's going to Manila to marry a woman he hasn't met but has been writing for two years. He is 41 and she is 22. He is "tired of taking crap" from American women. He is a sailor and his wife cheated on him.

On the plane, I sit beside a well-to-do Filipino woman who lives in Vancouver.

She is reading a *Cosmopolitan* article: *"Seven Little Things You can do to Make Good Sex Great."* Being in love isn't one of them.

Fourteen hours later, I change planes in Manila for General Santos, where I meet Cecilia and we fly to Devao and our old haunt, the *Insular Century Hotel.*

We hadn't seen each other for six weeks and, after two weeks, we may not be together again for months.

Yet a steady diet of sex for two weeks will make me sick of it. The sensible thing is to *pace* ourselves.

On the other hand, when I grew up it was *ungallant* for a man to deny a woman, (cf. *Zorba the Greek*). And self-discipline has never been my strong suit.

So instead, I adopt the policy of getting *really* sick of sex so I won't miss it for a least a month after. Between meals, walks and swims, we make love six times a day. Soon my interest is such that I can't respond.

Some males feel inadequate in these circumstances but I trust the judgment of my penis. Still I don't want to disappoint my soon-to-be bride. I enlist her help with some "turn on" games.

Cecilia gets very beautiful when she is angry. She is a natural actress. "Darling, pretend you are angry with me," I ask.

She glowers at me. She smolders. She's gorgeous. I imagine I am overcoming her reluctance. It works.

Afterward I ask, "How can you love such a pervert?'

"Because I am a pervert too," she answers.

Eureka!

I resolved not to make conversation an issue and indeed, it is forthcoming. "Didn't I tell you, I would speak to you if you didn't force me?" she says.

I question her again about her sexual experience. Cecilia insists she only hugged and kissed her former boyfriend but it turns out her studies weren't confined to psychology texts. Since the age of 11, she has been reading sexually explicit romance novels.

Changing the subject, I ask: "Were you really *afraid* to talk to me?" I find this incomprehensible since I lean over backward to please her. She says she was.

I give her a long pep talk about how we will compromise. Sometimes *my* way. Sometimes *your* way. Sometimes *half* way. But I will decide.

I ask why she never asks me questions about myself. She says she is curious but it is not her way to ask questions. I will tell her what I want her to know.

* * *

Before leaving Canada, I got stoned and had a mystical experience. We are *in love* all the time. God is Love. And we are *in God*.

When we fall in love, we are really discovering our true condition. When someone you love loves you, you've *broken through*.

I want to have this experience with Cecilia but after the long trip I feel tired and dull. I want to *break through* with her.

I start gulping down whiskey because I can get high this way. I find myself naked on my back in the bath size shower stall. Cecilia stands before me naked in the shower, a misty halo surrounds her gorgeous face and body.

The heart energy starts to flow.

"Beautiful faces aren't bone structure," I say to her. "Beautiful faces reflect beautiful souls. God gave you a beautiful soul and put it in your body."

'We worship God through his creation. I worship you Cecilia. My worship is my love."

"You are painfully beautiful. Excruciatingly beautiful. The most beautiful creature in the universe. I value you above everything in the world."

"Only things you cannot buy have any value. You are priceless."

"As of now, there is no other woman in the world. As far as I'm concerned, *No other woman exists*. You are the only woman in the world."

Isn't this the way to talk to God?

She laps it up. My words flow up to her in waves and she seems to wade into them.

Only I haven't been keeping track of the whiskey as I normally do. I vomit. Cecilia who has seen many college friends undergo this exorcism stands by me. I appreciate that she doesn't seem perturbed.

Afterward I can't remember a fraction of what I said but I feel in that shower, *we* were baptized.

* * *

Cecilia lets me read her diary for the period when we were apart. Perhaps she is making up for not talking to me. We are getting married in a couple of days and naturally I want to know as much about her as possible. It is illuminating.

Jan. 10, 1998: Is this my destiny?
To get married in early age (18 running to 19). I did not expect in my whole life that this will happen to marry a man of different tradition/nation and 30 years older than me but it doesn't matter for me any more 'coz I love him…

Jan 12, 1998: Papa Andy is very emotional.
I understand their feelings (my parents) I am their only child and they focused their attention to me. So it will be a difficult adjustment for them when I will get married. We'll have to face life that I will not stay with my parents forever….Help me Lord. I hope that I will not regret this decision for the rest of my life. I'm not looking/finding for the physical happiness but more on emotionally and spiritually most of all.

Jan 13, 1998: Sometimes I can't understand myself.
I committed myself to my dear Henry but I'm eager to see/meet Gerry. I like him in his letters and I thought I'm beginning to love him. We've been writing for more than two years and we treated each other as best of friends…shared everything with him…Although I have never met him, he has been my inspiration and I dreamed to be with him for the rest of my life. But here comes Henry. I didn't teach myself to love him because I just felt it naturally…I'm willing to take the gamble.

Love, you are very powerful. If you enter the heart, no one can help but follow you.

Jan 15, 1998: I won't change my mind.
Michelle, Elon and I talked about my pen pals and saw the picture of Allan [the Harvard MBA student] & read his letter & ask me. "What if you choose Allan instead of Henry?" I said no, I'm already committed to Henry & I won't change my mind. I love Henry. Michelle said at your age a lady is not stable and always changes her mind. I said not for me; once I already decide then no one could break it, could change it.

Jan 23, 1998: I'm afraid because Roland is desperate.
He told me he will never go to Manila without me with him. By hook or by crook he will get me. I said, "Find a woman that's deserving of your love. There are so many gals." He replied; "I can't find a woman like you & I want you to be the mother of my children." ..His love is great but I can't give him a chance 'coz I'm already taken....What if he'll make trouble on my wedding day?"

Jan 23: I was so upset with somebody...
She told me [Henry] is too old for you, he's like your father...I told her I don't want to look for a young man who's not mature (thoughts, decisions who will just hurt me, take advantage with me, disrespectful with me and with my parents. I will still choose Henry. He's a very fine man. I do admit that in first meeting I just like (not love)him. But I like him (Henry) in the way he's been to me... I never expected to have a future husband that is understanding, caring, thoughtful and loving as him.

* * *

Devao, Feb. 8, 1998
No premarital idyll would be complete without a good fight. Ours begins in the evening at a fruit stand in a downtown open market. I remark that some oranges are soft and refrain from buying them. I also fuss about the price of some "mango stans", an exotic fruit Cecilia buys. They cost a third as much as some shoes we just pur-

chased for her.

In the cab, Cecilia's face is a storm cloud and I am getting the silent treatment. I assume it's because of my churlish price complaints and apologize. But she doesn't relent. "Look I apologized," I say. "You must forgive me."

Silence.

"Talk to me!"

"I will tell you when we arrive at the hotel," she says.

Finally in our room, she says: "I did not want the taxi driver to know our trouble. You disrespected the woman at the fruit stand. She said bad things about you."

I later learned that in the East, keeping face in public is all-important. But I see this as an unfair and irrational attack from the person closest to me. I will not apologize.

"In my culture, saying the fruit is soft is not an insult," I explain.

"How can you respect the fruit lady more than your husband?"

She is unimpressed. Scowl and silent treatment continues.

"How can you take the fruit lady's side? Are you going to marry her?"

Silence.

"This is great Cecilia. The night before our marriage, you decide to show me how irrational you are!?"

And I continue to make her madder still.

"Thanks for proving that my sister is right. That you are a crazy teenager. You know it's still not too late for you to go home alone tomorrow. We don't have to get married."

I automatically bottom line things prematurely (and immaturely).

"I can go home alone tomorrow," she says.

And she would. Over my disrespecting the fruit lady. Call off the wedding.

I reason that she is all emotion and doesn't have control. She is a force of nature. I have to be the rational one. I switch course and start to "love her up."

After a few minutes, I get her to apologize for her behavior.

I tell her that she won't manipulate me. I have had enough of that in the past. If she has a problem, she has to tell me. No more silent treatment, OK? She promises.

In retrospect, Cecilia probably thought the fruit lady had been insulted and her own reaction justified. But I suspect she had to save face too. When I confronted her, she resisted. She could not back down. But when I was loving and conciliatory, so was she.

* * *

February 9, 1997

Maitum is far better in February than it was before Christmas. The atmosphere is more relaxed; it is not as hot and there are no fire-crackers. Cecilia's mother has stopped working for the neighbor and the house and yard are spiffy clean. We arrive from Devao at about 9.30 a.m. and by 11.30 a.m. we are married at the town hall. It's a for-mality. We have a reception meal at the Mayor's restaurant.

Now the fun part begins. Learning about my wife.

I am sitting on the front step with Andy smoking a cigarette. I ask why there is no food in the cooler.

He says there is no money for food. He hasn't had enough work. The local economy is suffering due to the El Nino draught. Even the rich neighbor, the rice wholesaler, might lose his house.

Didn't Cecilia give you any money? I ask. A little, he says.

Why didn't you ask her?

"I do not ask my daughter for money," he says. Talk about a proud man.

Can't she see there's no food? Doesn't she ask? Doesn't she want to know? Is she stupid?

"Stupid," he says.

"I'd go crazy if I thought about money," she told me later. So she doesn't.

I thought I was marrying a young woman accustomed to poverty and the harsh realities of life. But I discover she is so sheltered by her parents she might have been brought up in Beverly Hills.

I asked if she wanted to know how much money I had. She didn't. She said she would be content if I moved to Maitum and we lived there. We even looked at structures for sale that were no better than the one she lived in. She had seen pictures of my house.

I thought I was getting a down-to-earth peasant girl. Instead I married an impractical girl with an artistic temperament. She loves music, dancing and drawing. Maybe that's why I fell for her.

I tell Andy that I will instruct Cecilia to give him 4000 pesos each month (about $100 U.S.) which is enough for necessities. He says that he will save as much as possible toward buying a building lot.

As we are conversing, Cecilia discovers us smoking. When we refuse to put out our cigarettes, she takes one from the package, lights it and starts puffing.

I can't stand it. I put out my cigarette.

* * *

In a relaxed no pressure setting, Cecilia will talk to me spontaneously. The afternoon of our wedding day, we are hanging around her bedroom. She is exchanging braying sounds with a goat parked in the grass across the street.

We talk about our proudest and our most embarrassing moments. Her proudest moment was becoming the literary editor of her high school newspaper. This position gave her a chance to travel to workshops around the island.

Her most embarrassing moment was one day at college when she was the only one who didn't notice her professor enter the classroom. She went on chattering and eating for a full five minutes oblivious to the teacher's stern gaze.

Why do I find this kind of innocence so attractive?

I change the subject. She has a strong sex drive. In our long separation ahead, maybe two months, does she know about masturbation?

She knows about it but she won't.

First her dad won't ask his own daughter for money. Then she won't seek sexual pleasure detached from its source and inspiration. My reaction: Is this what they used to call "character"?

Why do we rarely hear about issues of character? Why are they so rarely the subjects of movies or songs? We are so compromised as human beings, we don't even know it. We don't know how much we've given up to our culture of self-seeking and money worship.

The world is in the grip of people in the grip of greed and we are brutally, severely compromised.

* * *

Python Eats Baby Alive in Cavite *(Philippine Star)*
A two-month-old baby was eaten by a python while sleeping in Bucal village in Cavite, police reported yesterday. Police said the baby Raul Bacalzo, was sleeping in the bedroom of his family home when the python allegedly crept into the room and ate him. The boy's mother, Marianne Lipos said she was making dinner when she heard her child cry. When checking on the infant, he had disappeared, she said. She then noticed the snake leaving the house through the kitchen exit and heading to the woods, she told police. The snake and the remains of the boy have not been found. The incident comes after a 32-year-old Mangyan tribesman, who left his home in Mindoro to hunt for bats, was found inside the belly of a python.

* * *

Cecilia wants to go to Baguio for our honeymoon. Baguio, a city in the mountains 250 kms north of Manila, is a popular destination because of its cool climate. After a couple of days in Maitum, we take a van to General Santos. Andy and Mely accompany us. Dressed in their Sunday best, armed with the bankbook, they are spending the day in the city. It's hard to tell *which* couple is on their honeymoon.

The five days we spend in Baguio quickly highlight the issues our young marriage faces. I feel off balance, falling into my old habit of trying too hard to please a woman.

For example, we are having more sex than I want. I should have stopped it but there is something gratifying about the second look a young wife gives you when you've performed with distinction. But after a couple of days of lovemaking, I am exhausted.

I have to draw a line.

The self sacrificing love I feel for Cecilia is not enough. It must be balanced by an equally ardent love of self. I need time to think, enjoy myself, commune with God, work.

Otherwise I become needy and dependent. I know I'm in trouble when I keep asking Cecilia to reassure me of her love. Besides, my self-sacrifice is spoiling Cecilia, making her think she can have anything she wants.

Saturday afternoon, I tell Cecilia I need to be alone. I don't have the energy to keep my promise to visit the Botanical Garden. By her reaction I can see I have already spoiled her. She doesn't say anything but her expression and demeanor convey big time disappointment and indignation.

With Cecilia fuming in the next room, there is no way I can relax and read the paper. I accuse her of acting like a spoiled child, throwing a tantrum when she doesn't get her way. I thought I was marrying a woman who would put me first. But at this moment, she seems as selfish as any woman I've met.

As usual I do everything wrong and the situation deteriorates. I demand she explain herself but she refuses. I give her an opportunity to apologize and make up but she pushes me away. Finally I do what I should have done in the first place. I leave.

I repair to a nearby coffee shop, smoke my cigarillo and contemplate the situation. I am an explorer in the undiscovered continent of love, a scientist in the laboratory of masculine longing. Can a middle-aged man, scarred by the sex wars at home, find a new beginning on a tropical island where women are still feminine? Things don't look so good at this moment. Is my hypothesis wrong? Or will it be discredited because I chose the *wrong* woman? I sense the satisfaction feminists would be feeling now. But I am not about to panic.

When I return, Cecilia is writing a letter to her best friend. She pushes me away and I threaten to leave for a longer time. Then I take her in my arms and explain that I need to be alone or I'll get weak. I explain my history. She seems to understand. I get her to apologize for her tantrum, though this concession is only made via eyebrows.

"Put my needs ahead of yours," I tell her. "I'm always anticipating your needs. I bring you music. I buy you eyeglasses and shoes. You don't need to ask. Don't just be a taker. *Put me first so I can put you first.*"

"Obey me and you'll be happy," I promise her. "I'm a good and just man, easy to obey." She seems content, smothering me with kisses like a big puppy.

In retrospect, I needed to ignore her reaction and go out. She is emotional and her disappointment passes quickly. She told me later that she was already considering alternatives when I started calling her selfish.

* * *

Saturday night I suggest we go to a nightclub. When it's nearly time to leave, without saying a word, Cecilia runs a bubble bath and settles in for a long engagement. So I go out alone, to a packed club where hundreds of young Filipinos are rollicking in their seats to the less memorable hits of 1974.

For the price of a beer, I have a revelation. Another reason I am *off balance* is that I am always initiating conversation. Asking the questions. Talking for two. *I can be silent too!*

Returning to the hearth, Cecilia is the picture of domesticity watching a movie in bed with a towel wrapped around her hair. She is glad to see me. She looks at me expectantly. I just smile and lie down and watch the movie. I can keep my counsel too. It feels good.

The movie is a lovely illustration of Filipino marital values. A Bavarian princess visiting Manila feels her life is empty without love. She escapes her official entourage and falls for a lowly Manila jeepney driver. By learning to cook Filipino food and to clean house, she slowly wins his heart. In one scene, he offers to carry two heavy pails of water but she insists on demonstrating her mettle to him.

Eventually her identity is exposed and the proud jeepney driver sends her away. Then he has a change of heart and finds her at an official function. Running to join him, she literally throws her gold watch and diamond jewelry to the crowds.

In the final scene, she is in the front of the jeepney helping her man collect fares. The movie is called "As Long As You Love Me" and stars Dayanara Torres (Miss Universe 1993) and Filipino heartthrob Aga Mulach. It should be in a video stores in a Filipino neighborhood near you.

* * *

Next morning I suggest we go to the Botanical Garden. Afterward, we attend a church service. The priest talks about the abomination of poverty, and how the rich rely on money for their security so only the poor are receptive to God.

During the service my mind is busy with my own dogma.

Man loves woman like God loves man.

Man proposes. God disposes. Man obeys God.

Woman proposes. Man disposes. Woman obeys man.

I tell Cecilia that I ask God but He decides and I don't protest.

She should tell me what she wants and accept my decision serenely. Naturally I will try to make her happy.

This is ironic in light of what happens at lunch.

We go to a Chinese restaurant and order three dishes. I am hungry but when I reach for the vegetables, Cecilia says they are just for her. Even though she knows I hate fish sauce, she ordered vegetables smothered with it.

I am taken aback. "How could you be so inconsiderate? Not even the most selfish woman in America would do that!"

She is upset.

Just apologize and we'll forget it, I say.

But she won't apologize and she won't eat. She's lost her appetite. The vegetables sit untouched. She won't talk to me. I finish my meal quickly and we leave.

Outside the restaurant, she reproaches me: "You raised your voice to me in public. You are the only man who has ever done that."

"You caught me off guard," I say. "I lost my temper. I couldn't believe you'd do that."

Another preconception is crumbling. I thought Cecilia would have been taught by her mother to put her husband first. But in many respects she seems to be as focused on her own satisfaction as any young woman anywhere.

My frustration builds late Sunday afternoon when, despite a moratorium, cuddling degenerates into another session of unsatisfactory (for me) sex.

I am beginning to feel like an appliance.

Finally, she is satisfied and goes to sleep without saying a word. It is 6 p.m.

Feeling intense dissatisfaction, I want to go into town. But in the darkened room, I can't find my wallet. When I turn on the light, she makes angry faces and noises.

So I wander around Baguio with only a few pesos in my pocket and imagine I am poor like the people around me. I count out 25 pesos for a bowl of soup and imagine it has to last a day. I lament how much of my confidence comes from that wallet.

When I return at 8 p.m., Cecilia is still sleeping. I've had enough. I turn on the light and wake her rudely. She is very sensitive to tone. She cringes beside the bed in the corner.

My frustration boils over. "How can you just go to sleep at 6 p.m. without considering me? What about supper? What about our evening? I am *always* considering you. When I just went out, I left a note telling you what to do if you are hungry."

I continue: "When I turned on the light, you should ask what is wrong. Don't just make angry sounds."

By this time, she is standing on a chair at the balcony railing and I wonder if she's going to jump. This is as weird as I've seen.

I ask if she's planning to jump. She says she isn't.

"I am *frightened*," I tell her. "I am frightened I married a spoiled selfish sheltered girl. When we get out of a taxi, you leave me to struggle with the packages. You should be thinking about how you can help me."

By this time she is kneeling on the balcony with her arms extended to each side praying to God. Is this par for a honeymoon?

I rail on: "See the trouble we're in now? I wanted to wait but you had to get married right away. You've got one choice, you can go home now and we'll sort it out later. Or you can conform to me."

I go into the bedroom and turn on the TV. After an hour, I look in on her. She is writing in her diary. I carry her to one of the beds.

An uncanny thing happens. This is definitely the *low* point of our relationship.

Yet weirdly I feel *closer* to her than ever. Although I was spent sexually, I feel an incredible desire *as I've never felt before*. I literally *ache* for her.

She returns my hug; it means she will conform to me.

"Teach me how to be a good wife," she says.

"Consider me first," I tell her. "I love you. I'm always thinking of your needs. So think of my needs. Put me first so I can put you first."

I ask her how I can be a good husband.

"Don't raise your voice," she says. "When you want to talk to me, talk to me nicely. Shouting at me doesn't work. If you have a temper, cool off first. If I am silent, ignore me."

* * *

A traditional wife is like a pet. *She won't leave you.* Writing in her diary at the height of our fight Sunday, Cecilia sees her options in terms of either sacrificing her whole life to an abusive man or becoming a nun. Leaving me for another suitor is not an option. On the balcony, with her arms outstretched, she was praying for a sign from God *to become a nun.*

"Lord I know you have really a purpose for my life," she writes. "I ask you if it is really meant for me to become a single blessedness [nun] then just show me the sign. I'm already afraid to be alone with him in Canada. But if it's really my destiny to sacrifice, well I'll take it Lord."

I kid her afterward: "What if the phone rang and it was the convent in Davao. They have an opening in the new class."

She just smiles.

"You're *my* nun now," I tell her.

In the same diary entry she laments the injustice of my accusations.

"What have I done to be accused as a self centered one. I even think of him every time. He said to me love is selfless. I'm not thinking of what I get if he needs time for himself. I'm trying my best to understand him."

She goes on. "He tells me I am a big gamble on his part. It is also a big gamble on my part. I have to give up the people who are closest to me – my friends, my parents to follow him."

* * *

The fights are like having a tooth removed: a painful but necessary adjustment to being a couple. Ultimately in marriage, two wills become one. (Isn't a child a beautiful expression of that unity?) But the mechanics of how two wills meld are not described in any engineering texts.

The fights take up only two of the seven days of our honeymoon. The rest of it was fine. Baguio felt congested and polluted. There are not a lot of public places in a third world country. The only park worth visiting was an old U.S. army base surrounded by a fence. We had to take a taxi to the entrance and back.

But we had a lovely suite with a beautiful view and spent much of our time there. Cecilia watched a lot of TV. She is a big basketball fan and had to see her favorite team *Alaska Milk* play arch rivals *Purefoods, Gordon Gin* and *Formula Shell*. She also caught up on sentimental Tagalog movies. One night she was crying over one about a mother and daughter. It reminded her of her birth mother whom she has never met.

We went to see "The Devil's Advocate". I took pleasure in the enjoyment evident on her face. Afterward she repeated Al Pacino's line with glee: "Vanity is definitely my favorite sin!"

One night when the compulsion to have sex had abated, Cecilia started talking freely. She told me that she had a recurrent dream of climbing a circular staircase. An old man on a landing tells her she can't go all the way up yet. She's not sure what is above. She also had a dream about going to the *Insular Century Hotel* before she actually went there. She was early and couldn't make out whom she was with.

I shared with her my realization that she is primarily an emotional person. What she is feeling in the moment is what she is. She kissed me, seeming to appreciate this perception from an otherwise obtuse man.

* * *

February 1998; Back in Canada
Canada is a place that makes me feel that the pursuit of anything other than money is totally feckless.

Remember how Andy and Mely looked like *they* were going on the honeymoon? Dressed in their Sunday best, the bankbook in Andy's pocket, something about this picture had disturbed me.

Cecilia phones to say that on that day Andy withdrew 10,000 pesos from the bank account and bought a television and a VCR. The time payments will add up to another 30,000 pesos. (40K pesos=$1000 US)

She had quarreled with her father. "You should have waited and consulted us," she told him. She couldn't sleep.

I am shocked. Andy is the epitome of integrity for me. I feel betrayed. I want to confront him. "The money is for necessities, not luxuries," I tell Cecilia. "Do you feel we were betrayed?"

"Sometimes it gets lonely here. . ." she ventures.

I discuss it with my dad. "Let it go," he tells me. "The TV is probably the only chance this man will get to see the outside world."

I discuss it with Todd. "Put Cecilia first," he advises. "She is caught between her father and her husband."

I eventually take Todd's advice.

* * *

The issue of the TV is swept away by the next phone call. Cecilia is crying. She has been bleeding continuously since the honeymoon and is weak and dizzy.

She has a "cyctetic cyst" on one ovary. If the medicine doesn't make the bleeding stop, there will be an operation to remove the cyst. She is afraid of dying.

She calls again a few days later. She has been to another doctor who has made a different diagnosis. She will be ok. She's been to a wedding with a friend and she's all sunny.

But the bleeding doesn't stop. I am worried and promise to return to the Philippines in two weeks. She cries with joy. No one has ever cried with joy about seeing me in my life.

In the interim, the doctor discovers that Cecilia has had a miscarriage. Ten days before I arrive, she has a DNC. There was no fetus, just placenta. She doesn't suffer a feeling of loss.

Chapter Eight

Third Trip: Joining Your Life With Someone You Don't Really Know

April, 1998.

Cecilia and her mother are sitting on a planter when I exit the airport at General Santos. She looks wan but on glimpsing me has a physical reaction of relief. Her mother looks so dopey, I ask Cecilia if anything is wrong. "Just tired, we got only four hours sleep," she says.

We hop a Beechcraft for Davao and the *Insular Century Hotel*. The purpose of this trip is to get a tourist visa so we can be together in Canada while the immigration visa is processed. The first step is to get a Philippine passport, which requires numerous documents and an interview. That's why we are in Davao again.

The week passes uneventfully. Sex, sleep, food. Cecilia is still recovering from the operation and I am recovering from jet lag. I don't try to resist my young wife's sexual demands.

Returning to the hotel room one day, I fumble with the keys. "Which key is for you?" I tease her.

She points to my penis. So true.

I've figured out the purpose of the incessant lovemaking. Certainly my appetite is not that great. This is as good a place as any to say, I don't usually come. It just makes me tired. I enjoy giving Cecilia pleasure. My reward is the expression on her face. She is so beautiful at these times. I am a musician. Her beauty is the music. It nourishes my soul.

The unconscious purpose of all this sex is bonding. Her body is imprinted on my being. When I return to Canada I feel grounded: the energy has found it's channel. I am not attracted to other women. Nevertheless I do try to add variety to our time together. I give her a book of card games and ask her to find a game that two people can play.

When I return from the bathroom, she is in the middle of a game of Solitaire with the cards spread out all over the bed. Solitaire! *This seems like the epitome of her self-centered myopia.*

I must be run-down from all the sex, because I blow up at her, call her stupid, insensitive, selfish and storm out. When I return she is gone but there is this note on the bed.

Don't worry about me. I'm only in the seashore. Just wait for me here ok. I was shocked when you were angry. You said to me you'll talk to me in a nice way. You could say to me ok Ceci stop that solitaire & we could have the game now. Remember you said to me you'll talk to me nicely if there's something wrong. Don't just burst out....You don't see me shouting at you, saying words that could hurt your feelings... I hope you forgive me if it's my mistake. I love you. Ceci

* * *

Waiting. People in the Third World spend more time waiting. After a couple of hours at the crowded passport office, Ceci gets her precious passport. To celebrate, we take the two travel agents that assisted us out for a meal. They want to go to McDonald's.

Both these young women have four-year university degrees. In the Philippines, you need a university degree to get any job beyond sales clerk. They earn only $120 a mos. Ed, Cecilia's friend, is studying to be a civil engineer. He expects to earn only $200 US a month.

The two travel agents are in their early twenties. I win their lifelong affection by assuring them that in America, unlike the Philippines, they would still be considered of prime marrying age, even a little young. I ask them if they believe in obeying their husbands. "Yes" they eagerly reply.

Passport in hand, Cecilia and I fly to Manila to see about a visitor's visa at the Canadian Embassy. After waiting three hours and paying $75, I am told Cecilia cannot visit me in Canada because they can't remove her if her immigration visa is denied.

I show the embassy official some recent newspaper stories that say Mindanao could erupt in bloody civil war at any moment. He admits it would look bad if she was killed but he is not prepared to grant us our request.

Nevertheless, he compensates by opening an immigration file for Cecilia even though the sponsorship won't arrive for another six weeks. He gives us the forms for a medical exam, a process that would have delayed her visa for a couple of months. The medical is completed.

As well, we brave Manila traffic jams to reach the Philippine equivalent of the FBI where Cecilia is fingerprinted, palm printed and otherwise screened for a security clearance. So the trip to Manila wasn't a total waste.

From Manila we return to Ceci's home in Maitum where we spend a week. The TV set and VCR are the centerpiece of the living room which has only stools and a bench. In retrospect, I'm glad I didn't make an issue. Andy says it is lonely when Cecilia is gone.

"Sometimes Mely and I just sit on the front step in the evening and look at each other with nothing to say." I pay off the balance owing on the TV and VCR.

I have brought six videos. *Map of the Human Heart, Flirting* and *Delores Claiborne* are the most popular.

"Your attitude toward the TV changed." Andy says to me.

"I don't believe families should fight over money," I reply.

One night after watching *Green Card*, Cecilia says: "My parents are watching a Tagalog movie and having fruit. I want to join them."

I am not even given the courtesy of refusing an invitation.

"Fine," I say. "You can do your thing but don't wake me afterward for *anything*. I'm going to sleep."

But sure enough, when that treat is over, Cecilia comes to bed and wants another. I was asleep. This kind of excess bothers me. You can't have it all and I tell her so.

She will settle for a hand job.

"OK but I haven't got all night. If you haven't come in 10 minutes, I'm stopping."

"Twenty minutes," she counters.

Beggars can't be choosers.

"It's not feminine to demand sex. Don't ever do it again. You can indicate an interest but if I say no, stop."

"Is that the same for you?" she asks.

"Yes. When you say you're serious, I stop."

But she is not satisfied. She gets out of bed and sits brooding on the windowsill.

Alarm bells are going off in my head. I'm afraid her sexual demands are a clue to her character. I accuse her of being a selfish stubborn woman.

"A woman who is selfish is not a woman." I say. "Why would a man love and work for someone who is selfish? A woman should be devoted to her husband and children. Then they will love and cherish her."

Cecilia doesn't respond. Things degenerate as usual. I threaten to leave if she doesn't come back to bed. Finally, the sight of me actually packing rouses her from the windowsill and she returns to bed. The post fight energy kicks in and she gets what she wanted in the first place.

But I am disappointed in her. I question my feelings for her. Cecilia's home, formerly a palace, becomes a hovel in my mind. I wonder what I am doing there.

* * *

The next day she sleeps in and when she awakes, she has abdominal pains. It is not her period. I am not sympathetic at first. God, it's one thing after another, I think.

Her mother takes her to the home of a traditional healer. The healer's whole extended family – mother, daughters, son-in-law, and grandchildren — are present as she administers lotions and massages. A duck and ducklings poke their heads in the door. A tiny lizard jumps over my lap.

"This is what life is all about," I muse. I was single until the age of 32 and practiced a yogic asceticism. "Don't love people. Love God, and you will never be hurt," yogis preach.

This, I now realize, is garbage. God is Creation and we were put here to love Creation. You choose people to love and you stand by them, for better or for worse. The alternative may be painless but it is death.

 Finally Cecilia is feeling better and we return to the house.

The fact that I came along and stood by her makes Cecilia open up. She explains that this is an ongoing ailment called "pasma" in Tagalog. It is related to being exposed to extremes of hot and cold and it is not recognized by western medicine.

She's had it since she was a college student. When it struck, she'd rush to her boarding house. She'd have to walk in the heat because there was no transportation on campus.

This image awakens my protective instincts.

"You need someone to look after you, don't you?"

She looks at me tentatively.

 "Say it," I urge her.

"Henry, I need you to look after me."

I find this immensely satisfying.

"I get so sad when you act selfishly. I think you don't *really* love me."

"Why?"

"People in Canada think this is economic."

Urgently, gently, she embraces me.

 "It's *not*."

Then she says: "Don't say you'll leave when we fight. What if I let you?"

"I'll go."

"No."

"Then how do I make you obey me?

"I told you. Caress me."

* * *

Yin and yang. Man is the farmer. Woman is the earth. I will plow your furrows. I will plant my seed.

* * *

Talking to Andy

"Getting married is the most stressful thing a man can do," I tell him.

"Why?"

"You are joining your life with someone you don't really know."

"When I got married," he says, "I decided to rely on myself."

"What do you mean?"

"Whatever happens, I will accept it."

"And how has it been?"

"We don't talk much. We work. We help each other. We are happy."

* * *

Love. We have forgotten how to love in the West.

It's all barter. Security. Sex. Titillation. No wonder we are so cynical about love. Love. Such an impractical thing. It can't be measured or weighed. Easy to forget it exists. Seems silly to seek it. Except, without it, life is hollow and senseless.

Once, sitting together on her bed, Cecilia, unbidden, kissed my face. Not my lips. My face. Once. That's where I have always wanted to be kissed.

"Do they have homes for the aged in Canada?" she asked.

Yeah. Why?

"They don't have them here in the Philippines. Families take care of that."

Then, looking at me, a loving expression on her beautiful face, this 18-year-old said.

"I want to look after you when you are old."

* * *

I'm back in Canada. Cecilia calls in tears. Her father has thrown her out of the house because she has been disrespectful. I tell her she must obey her father as long as she lives there. Go back and apologize.

"Do you still love me even though you know I have problems?" she asks.

We all have problems, I reply.

Andy's problem was about to become mine.

Chapter Nine

I Married a Teenager

Xmas 1999.

Cecilia has been here five months. I haven't written because I wasn't sure this marriage was going to work. I have often regretted marrying Cecilia and wasn't going to complete this diary of love, let alone publish it. Things have gone desperately wrong and I don't know why.

First, Cecilia arrived on August 1, 1998 with a menstrual disorder. She had lost so much blood, she almost needed a transfusion. It took more than a month and excellent free Canadian medical care for her to recover.

I attributed our problems to her immaturity. God knows, I saw it all in the Philippines; but when I set my heart on something, I am a master of denial.

I overestimated her maturity because sexually she was a woman. I expected her to fit my preconception of a traditional, submissive woman, as she said she would. But in a country full of such women, I *would* choose one brimming with the conceit of youth (i.e. immaturity).

The young want too much, they give too little and they don't appreciate what they have. Also known as "teenagers," they are deceptively adult-like in appearance but in fact, live parasitically off of society. Four-letter words to them are *give* and *help*.

I was not aware of this common affliction because I was never young myself. I read *The Rise and Fall of The Third Reich* when I was ten and spent my teenage years pondering its implications. I worked as a columnist and reporter from the age of eleven.

I mistakenly assumed a girl from a poverty-stricken background would be used to working, and would appreciate what I gave her. Trust me to choose an adopted only child, spoiled and sheltered by her parents. Trust me to find one whose father was so capable, he did much of the housework, setting a bad example.

The first five months have seen a major readjustment in my expectations.

Take work for example. Cecilia hadn't done a day's work in her life. Around her father's house, she was a teenager: messy and lazy. She was used to sleeping in, listening to music, writing letters and seeing friends.

I wanted her to get a job to develop character and pride. She could keep her earnings and support her parents like she said. But she proved to be incapable of working.

The local supermarket offered to train her but she got bored and quit. The owner said she was slow and lacked initiative. Cecilia volunteered at a childcare center. The children liked her but her supervisor said she lacked the competence to take charge of children.

We visited the local hairdressing and esthetician schools but these professions seemed too arduous and insecure.

If she couldn't work, I tried to find other activities and friends. I arranged piano and dance lessons. She became disenchanted with them. The new keyboard gathered dust.

She didn't seek friends in the city's 45,000 strong Filipino community. Winnipeg has the largest proportion of Filipinos of any city outside the Philippines. Cecilia considered joining the traditional dance troop but decided against it. Filipinos were nosey, gossipy and jealous, she said. As a result, she had few friends and this put a strain on me.

But some things were still in our favor. I wasn't mistaken about her love. Souls don't lie. She was gorgeous and thought I was sexy. She was affectionate and wanted me every day.

But most important, her love felt unconditional. I didn't have to jump through hoops to impress or keep her. She was mine. I could be myself, do what I wanted.

She loved good movies and could tell the difference. She'd be channel surfing and stop to watch Lina Wertmuller's *Swept Away*. We enjoyed many great movies together.

She got my jokes. When I said, "Beauty is only skin-deep, you taught me that," she burst out laughing. After a fight, I remarked on her irrationality because her period wasn't due. "Fasten your seatbelt!" she said.

After three weeks, I emailed a friend: *"Cecilia expresses herself mostly by facial expression. I do miss verbal communication. My fantasy is to meet a woman my age, tie her up, and have a conversation.*

On the plus side, there is no need for Viagra in this household. It's too early to say whether this marriage was folly or genius. I veer back and forth."

* * *

Our major problems were her stubborn temperament and her violent behavior.

Her father said she was "spoiled and immature." He gave her everything she wanted. If he didn't, she used to take a stick and beat it against the wall until he gave in.

I thought her teeth were a superficial flaw that I should ignore. In fact, they were a warning sign that I missed. They were bad because Andy spoiled her with candy. Her character could not be fixed as easily as were her teeth.

She got into a fury if I criticized her, or denied her anything. Four weeks after Cecilia's arrival, I again e-mailed my friend:

Cecilia and I had a big fight yesterday when I didn't immediately agree to fork out $100 for a Filipino party. I hesitated and said, we'll see. I've had a lot of expenses related to her, including buying her father a plot of land in the Philippines. She didn't say anything but her expression exuded such anger and disdain that I got annoyed. One thing led to another and I bottom-lined it: be a submissive wife like you promised or go back to the Philippines. All she heard was the latter part and she *pulled out her suitcase and started packing. I went for a walk and was planning to call a travel agent. But, when I returned, she was waiting at the window like a puppy and her expression denoted a change of heart. We are still enjoying the afterglow from making up.*

After Halloween, I attended a parent-teacher night with Josh and his mom. Cecilia wanted to join us. I said she couldn't come. When we returned, we found the pumpkin smashed to pieces on the front walk.

I couldn't go to a store with Cecilia without having a fight if I didn't buy her something. Her demands were sometimes unreasonable. When I bought a new computer, so she could have mine, she demanded and got the new one.

Once we went to a park to play Frisbee. When she didn't like the park, we went to another one. She didn't like it any better. She must have been PMS. Back at home, I said she was spoiled and crazy: "How can you object to a park?"

She responded by clearing hundreds of books from the shelves. Before she could trash the rest of the house, I pinned her on the carpet. She cursed me in English and Tagalog. "Fuck you, fuck you, fuck you!"

While this was happening, my son arrived for a visit. She wouldn't let me open the door. She wedged herself between it and a wall. Josh understood we couldn't meet. Through a window, he saw us in turmoil and all the books on the floor.

Another fight was about Andy. When he phoned, I learned that he had spent $500 on *Tupperware*. (Filipinos are often victimized by door to door salesmen.) I gave him the money for food. "Cecilia will inherit the Tupperware," he said.

My frustration must have shown. Cecilia ignored me for a day because I had been disrespectful. I decided to ignore her back and things got pretty grim. Luckily Andy called the next night and I patched things up to Cecilia's satisfaction.

Once, while doing her nails on the carpet, she spilled red nail polish. She flew into a rage because I was upset with her. She threw everything in the bathroom on the floor and dumped shampoo on the floor. As usual, I had to clean up the mess.

Generally, she showed anger and got her way by smashing a wine bottle (once), repeatedly slamming and kicking doors, throwing objects against the wall, turning up the stereo, trashing my office, ripping up business documents, starting fires, overturning furniture, and threatening to ransack or burn the whole house.

* * *

Our encounter with the champions of abused women began innocently enough one Sunday morning. Cecilia was jealous of Josh who had spent the night. She punched me in the shoulder, "to get my attention." After Josh left, I was irritated with her.

She replied by turning the 32" stereo TV up to top volume. I couldn't stand it. I kept turning it down and she kept turning it up. My attempts to reconcile failed. After many warnings, I forcibly evicted her from the house. She fought me tooth and nail.

It was an autumn Sunday and some neighbors witnessed the scene as Cecilia emerged crying. Cecilia, like a baby, knew the effect of crying and used it.

"It isn't what it looks like," I told the neighbors. I asked them to look after her. After a few hours, tempers cooled and she came home. We made up and discussed how to avoid fights. That night we went bowling with Josh. Things returned to normal.

Wednesday night, two policemen knocked on our door. They wanted to speak to Cecilia and I separately. One of the neighbors had informed them of our fight providing details Cecilia had given. If this happens to you, don't admit anything and call a lawyer.

Under the "zero tolerance" policy, any physical contact constitutes domestic assault. Although Cecilia didn't press charges, the police did. I was arrested.

In the police car, the constable said he had no discretion in the matter. He recognized that Cecilia was not in jeopardy. Cecilia ran across the snow to the police car in her nightgown and begged them in tears not to arrest me. We assured her that everything would be all right.

At the police station, I was kept in a cell for a couple of hours, booked and fingerprinted. I had to sign an undertaking to stay away from Cecilia and my house. If I had obeyed, I would not have been able to carry on my business. I had nowhere to go. No clothes. No tooth brush. I went home.

In court I pleaded guilty and received probation. I was required to take an "anger management course." There, I was treated as a chronic wife abuser, and my protests meant I was in denial. We were taught to take "time outs" (leave) when a fight starts. This was impossible in my case because Cecilia would block the door or threaten to trash the house if I left.

My officious neighbor assuaged her conscience by calling the authorities instead of speaking to us first. Similarly, Filipino "friends" invited Cecilia over one Sunday and convinced her to enter the local battered women's shelter. Their concern for her safety didn't extend to taking her in themselves. They never called her again.

Cecilia phoned and I picked her up. The counselor tried to convince her to divorce me and offered her help to get support payments. Apparently, heterosexual marriages are an affront to the womyn who run these shelters.

Cecilia's boredom and frustration grew. The onset of winter gave her the idea of returning to the Philippines for two months "to find herself." I toyed with the idea ending the marriage while she was there. I was afraid to tell her to her face.

Nevertheless, I leveled with her: I didn't want her to go home. If she went, I didn't want her back. I had had a new insight. *Love is not meant to be easy. It 's work.*

Loving Cecilia was my work. I would nurture her to maturity, teach her to set goals and achieve them. In the New Year, she'd take a course to become a Health Care Aide and learn to drive. We'd pursue our goals together.

I affirmed my love for her. I told myself, a woman wants to be loved and given a wholesome vision of life. The man must provide the leadership.

* * *

August, 2000.

Our major problem remained her violent behavior. I was afraid of her. Like thousands of other men, thanks to the zero tolerance policy, I was an abused husband.

Despite my efforts, we had another run-in with the law. One evening after I made supper as usual, I asked Cecilia to empty the dishwasher. She asked me to help her. Frustrated, I said: "Can't you *do anything*? Don't you want to help?" This was all it took.

She attacked me with both her fists. Then she threw everything from the counters and table onto the floor. She threw food at the wall. I restrained her on the carpet and she pretended to be hurt. "Fuck you, fuck you, fuck you," she spewed in English followed by curses and expletives in Tagalog. She could be pretty ugly at these times.

After a while, a phone call distracted her long enough for me to go to a movie.

When I returned, Cecilia was still talking happily on the phone. I went to bed. Then, she started kicking the door.

Bang. Bang. Bang. Attempts to reconcile were fruitless. Finally, I made the mistake of threatening to call the cops. "You can't terrorize me; they'll make you stop," I said.

But Cecilia had been to the *Women's Advocacy Group*. "I'll teach you a lesson," she said. "You'll be the one to go to jail." Of course she was right. I was on probation.

I spent the next hour begging her to change her mind. I pulled the phone from the wall and she tried to wrestle it from me. I told her our marriage would be over, and urged her not to be rash. Instead she ripped up a large photo of us.

She was determined to "teach me a lesson". Finally, I just gave up.

I should have been suspicious of her devil-may-care attitude but I attributed it to emotion and immaturity. Incidentally, this "lesson" would cost me $2600 in legal fees.

Six cops in three patrol cars arrived with flashing lights, answering the call of the victimized woman. We stood together on the porch, calmly waiting for them. We charged each other with assault and were taken downtown and held in separate cells.

After about three hours, Cecilia was again taken to the shelter for abused women. I was brought to the Winnipeg Remand Center, a downtown14-floor reflective glass tower, half filled with husbands.

* * *

Jail is an experience I am grateful for. I was held with sixty other men in a "range" with a large common space and about forty separate cells on two floors.

I was there for 30 hours because I delayed getting a lawyer. I thought I would be released if I explained what really happened. But, in a videoconference, a judge said he wasn't interested in what happened. He advised me to get a lawyer or I would be there for two weeks.

Prison taught me the value of freedom. I'll never take it for granted again. I missed the little things like being able to go for a walk, or make a cup of coffee.

I spent my time meditating. I now understood the meaning of power. It is a big club called "the law." Zero tolerance has given it to people who are PMS once a month. I vowed to campaign to change this grotesque policy which makes marriage a perilous enterprise for men.

My first bunkmate was a handsome West Indian fellow, about 25. He slapped his pregnant fiancée when she said she wanted an abortion. Did he deserve to be in jail? He introduced me to a friend who pushed his girlfriend out of his apartment. She wasn't living there.

I also met a Native Indian man whose wife had just given birth to their 13th child. She had him incarcerated for threatening, while drunk, to throw her through a wall. I could see the pain on his ancient face.

There were pay phones in the range. After my rage cooled, I forgave Cecilia. She was repentant and waited for me at home. She had no money and was barely able to fend for herself.

I appeared in court in prison dress — leg shackles and handcuffs — and was released later that day. After just 30 hours of incarceration, I identified with my fellow inmates. I was an insider. People on the street were "outsiders." The cold January air tingled with *freedom*!

I bought a newspaper and went to my favorite falafel place. What a pleasure!

At home, Cecilia greeted me with great emotion. We had torrid sex and resumed our routine. But when she mentioned visiting the Philippines again; of course, I didn't object. I was relieved to see her go.

When she phoned, I said I didn't want her back. She cried and promised to change. Foolishly, I gave her *one last chance*. Returning to Winnipeg on February 15, 1999, Cecilia was a changed woman. She was reasonable and did her share of the chores. This lasted for a day and a half.

She began the Health Care Aide course. She often refused to do her homework so I found myself preparing menus and short papers. For six weeks during her "practicum", I dragged her out of bed at 6.30 a.m., made breakfast, packed lunch and drove her to nursing homes.

In spite of my efforts, she missed many days, some due to sickness. She was put on probation. Somehow, Cecilia graduated in June 1999.

She quickly found a job at a modern nursing home. I would pick her up at midnight when the evening shift ended. When this beautiful girl in her smart new uniform emerged laughing and talking, tears of love and pride formed in my eyes.

* * *

To earn extra money, Cecilia accepted an extra shift; then, she was too tired to go.

I warned her she would be fired. She didn't care. Over her protests, I got her into the car. On the way, she opened the door and threatened to jump out. I had no alternative but to return home. I called her supervisor and didn't pretend she was ill. I told them the truth. She was fired.

Cecilia was now free to spend 16 hours a day on the Internet. I insisted she go to sleep at 1 a.m. This was literally the only demand I made of her. I couldn't sleep with her typing. We had many altercations. She'd kick over furniture but eventually she'd go to bed.

She sent her photo to 50 guys she met online. Their addresses are still on the computer. The phone began to ring with calls from her "friends." She behaved as though she wasn't married. She assured me it was harmless and I wanted to believe her. I chalked it up to her boundless female vanity.

How many suitors would satisfy you? I asked her once.

"A million," she said. Her purpose in life was to attract the maximum possible male attention.

She would primp half-naked in front of a mirror for hours. She'd smear a bleaching cream ("Porcelana") on her skin, and ask me over and over again: "Am I white? Am I whiter than those Filipinas we saw at the mall?"

Despite our problems I still regarded her as my wife and wanted to show her a good time. In the summer of 1999, we flew to Ottawa to see my dad. Then we rented a car and drove to Montreal. I took her to a fancy restaurant and showed her the sights. On the top of Mount Royal, she asked for an ice cream cone. I had been trying to wean her off this habit of asking me to buy her candy. I suggested she buy the cone herself.

That did it. She shut down and wouldn't move or speak to me. I relented but it was too late. After an hour of this, I'd had enough. We started back to Ottawa. On the freeway, she wanted to go back to Montreal. When I refused, she started pummeling me with both fists. *Then, she threw the gears into reverse.*

I was expecting an accident with damage to the car. Luckily, the Ford engineers foresaw this. To my surprise and relief, nothing happened.

I bought peace by promising to take her to a resort on the route back. As we crossed the river on a ferry, I asked her what she'd do if I divorced her. She couldn't fend for herself. She didn't seem too concerned.

When we got back to Winnipeg, I broke down in tears of frustration over the ruined vacation. Cecilia didn't even make a pretense of consoling me. She just logged on to the Internet. Frankly, I didn't know what to make of her.

Later that summer, I took her to a resort near Winnipeg. At night she was watching a horror movie I didn't like. To prevent me from going for a walk, she started to ransack the room. I was her prisoner. The next day she explained she was afraid of watching the movie alone.

On another occasion, she insisted I send more money to her parents. I had already sent a lot and wanted to give her some incentive to work. But it was easier for her to extort money from me. She started punching me, trashing my office and setting papers on fire.

I gave her a letter saying I intended to divorce her. She just ripped it up. I had no option but to wire the extra money. I considered going to the police but thought better of it.

Thanks to zero tolerance, I was continually terrorized and blackmailed. Cecilia was never in any danger from me. I had gone to the Philippines for a submissive woman and ended up powerless and abused.

The Internet was my savior, my baby sitter. True she was flirting with every male on the planet. But the alternative would have been for me to find her other diversions. The Internet enabled me to avoid confrontations and to work. I was preparing to teach a course at the university.

Some days I only saw her when she came out for meals or to take phone calls. Then I would suggest a driving lesson. But she was only interested in the Internet. There, she downloaded many useful programs. She wanted a camera so she could broadcast her image live to the world.

In July, Cecilia was offered a job earning $400 per week looking after a rich old lady. Often, on overnight shifts, she was able to sleep. But, after a month, she was fired when she refused to work a day shift. On days, her incompetence would have become evident, anyway.

* * *

Despite all this I was often surprisingly content with Cecilia. *Three* good qualities out of *five* weren't bad, I reasoned. The three points in her favor: sex, beauty and love. The two strikes against her: lazy and violent.

The arithmetic changed in late August when I opened a letter she wrote to her "friend" Gerry. I immediately recognized the style she reserved for the person she "loved": "Ever dearest. I love you. Miss you etc. etc."

I was shocked. I suddenly realized that her behavior wasn't simply due to immaturity. She wasn't trying. She was planning to divorce me and marry Gerry. She had no interest in making our marriage work. On the contrary, she wanted it to fail. That's why she put me in prison. She's probably not the first cheating wife who, thanks to zero tolerance, put a loyal and loving husband in jail.

Idealistic fool, I missed all the signs. Before coming here, she asked if she could visit Gerry. I said no. The request was troublesome to me but I stupidly assumed she obeyed. After her first month here, she ran up $500 in telephone calls to the Philippines. These calls were made at night while I was asleep. She said Gerry was giving her advice on how to adjust to married life. In addition, Gerry's letters were addressed to her maiden name. When I asked about this, she replied: "Don't interfere with my friendships." She said she told Gerry she was married and I stupidly believed her. She said he was disappointed but understood.

I confronted her with the letter. She said the loving remarks are typical of the "brotherly" quality of Filipino relationships. I didn't buy it.

Gerry was going to be on leave in the Philippines in September. She wanted to visit him and expected me to pay for the trip. I resisted but when she started to trash the house, I gave in. I had a plan. Secretly, I removed one of her return tickets. Goodbye Cecilia! Needless to say, her send-off at the airport lacked warmth and sincerity.

Indeed, I had agonized over serving her with a divorce petition at the departure gate. I carefully briefed a process server. But I called it off afraid she'd have a tantrum at the airport and refuse to leave. Getting rid of her was my first priority.

While she was away, I almost moved to an apartment. I wanted to hide in case she returned. Thanks to the zero tolerance policy, I was seriously traumatized by this 105 lb. woman I had rashly married. In the last minute, I decided she wouldn't drive me from my home.

I searched her stuff and found dozens of Gerry's letters. He didn't know she was married. She told him (and her other suitors) that I was her uncle. They were planning their wedding from the day she arrived in Canada.

* * *

Cecilia spent 10 days with Gerry in Manila. After she left for Maitum, I phoned Gerry. Cecilia had given me his number because presumably she wanted him to learn the truth and couldn't tell him herself. He was incredulous and demanded to see our marriage certificate. When it arrived, he was angry and agreed to sign an affidavit of adultery.

Cecilia called from Maitum. She had had unprotected sex with Gerry and had missed her period. In addition, a visitor to the house had stolen most of her money. I told her Gerry knew the truth and was finished with her. In that case, she didn't care about him and would return to Winnipeg.

If you're pregnant, you need to marry Gerry, I said. Imagine if she returned home pregnant with Gerry's kid!

I had a moral dilemma. If I didn't mention her missing ticket, she would be stranded in Manila without funds or friends. By this time, Gerry would have returned to the provinces. She had betrayed and exploited me. This would have been fitting revenge.

When I told her about the ticket, she burst into tears and begged me for help. "You're killing me," she kept repeating. "I have no life here anymore. I don't know what to do."

I had her where I wanted her. But, again, I took pity. I told her to go back to Manila immediately. Gerry would forgive her and help her deal with the airline. However, I didn't send the missing ticket.

In the end, Cecilia wasn't pregnant. Her period had been delayed by worry. Gerry borrowed $1200 and sent Cecilia back. I met her at the airport with the process server. She signed an affidavit of adultery so we could get a speedy divorce.

* * *

Cecilia tried to put our relationship on a new honest footing. She told me she secretly visited Gerry in July 1998, *a week before coming to Canada*. She was introduced to his parents as his future bride.

Recently, I found his letter to Cecilia dated July 17,1999: "*When will we celebrate our anniversary? If I'm not mistaken it's July 24, 1998 when we first met and I was already kissing you then but you only said you love me too the next day."*

She said Gerry often called her here (using a false name) and at her college. He refers to one such call in the same letter:

"One more thing that made me feel like a sick is that the third time I called your home, the one answering the phone whoever bastard that was told me that he was your husband and that – 'why I'm still interested in you where in fact you're already married.' It's unbelievable but it's good we're on the phone only otherwise I will punch him. It's not a good joke but then I was thinking it is possible to happen. How if one day you will tell me 'I'm sorry Ger but they forced me to marry him.' I'm praying it won't happen & I'm aware you won't do that."

Cecilia also admitted she stole $2000 from my wallet over the previous year, about $40 a week. This was in addition to the money I gave her. I had noticed cash was missing but she always denied taking it. If I had made an issue, I could have ended up in jail again.

She also said she didn't speak to me sometimes for fear of letting her deception slip out.

* * *

I wrote Andy about Cecilia's infidelity and her violent behavior. I blamed him for letting her marry and asked him to keep her in Maitum. Cecilia intercepted and burned these letters. But, after she left for Manila, one got through.

Andy phoned and asked for money to go to Manila and "advise" Cecilia. I hung up on him. Later he wrote to accuse me of being "jealous" of Gerry and of breaking my promise to give his daughter a good life.

So much for the "sanctity" of marriage, "character," "trust" and "tradition."

* * *

The last ten weeks with Cecilia were relatively stable. With the divorce pending, she had to behave herself. Finally, we were "on the same page." We both wanted her to find a new husband. She dumped Gerry because he was too beholden to his parents who now objected to her.

She spent her days trolling the Internet for a new husband. The phone rang constantly, day and night, as a dozen suitors competed for her hand. I gave them Billboard Magazine rankings: "Moving from #6 last week, to #3, Ron from New York."

She chose a personable 38-year-old Filipino in the American navy in San Diego. She met him in a chat room while he was stationed in Italy.

I helped her get the U.S. Visitor's Visa. On the night she left, I warned her she was dressed for a party, not a trip. She didn't listen and was refused entry. I had to go back to the airport and convince the official that she was my wife, and was coming back. She missed the plane, but got out the next night, in time to celebrate the Millennium New Year in her new home.

Cecilia said it was only a visit but I suspected (and hoped) she would not return.

* * *

In spite of our impending divorce, she occasionally phoned and mentioned coming back.

"I'm not running a hotel," I told her. "You belong with your sailor."

As it happened, there wasn't much danger. In May, she admitted she was four-months pregnant. After a few delays, our divorce came through. Cecilia remarried on June 6, a few days shy of her 21st birthday.

Her husband e-mailed me: "Thanks a lot for the assist in getting all the documents to her on time for us to finalize our union. Cecilia is doing fine and her tummy is getting bigger now."

I can't deny that I felt a twinge on learning she was married to someone else.

Some small part of me hoped she'd return. But on the rational level, I did not want her back. Who would?

* * *

Obviously, I was a stepping stone for her.

She was a stepping stone for me, too. I matured 15 years in the two I knew her. I don't know how I got to be 48 and remained so immature. I do know that thanks to Cecilia, I have finally lost the lifelong habit of feeling "unloved."

Sexually and emotionally, I compensated for time I spent as a young man reading and thinking instead of living and loving.

On some deep psychic level, we men need to earn our "pilot's license."

We need to log 2000 hours of *intensive sex*. One thousand hours should be spent looking at the dials and gauges of the face. Another thousand hours should be spent flying without instruments, "in the dark" with only moans and whimpers for direction.

The second part of the training is most important. As men, we need to demystify the "pot of gold" which so fascinates and compels us.

We need to discover that the pot of gold is, in fact, a pail of fish, with hair. An efficient and busy portal, it deserves respect but *not* adulation. After that, the rest of the female falls into perspective.

Luckily for my psychic development, Cecilia's youthful greed extended to sex. She was always ready and willing, two excellent qualities in a wife. Often she took the initiative. Every man craves the liberating experience of "possessing" a beautiful young woman, at least for a time. It's liberating partly because, when I had it, I realized it wasn't worth the trouble. I could live without it. At the end, our sex felt to me like masturbation.

But Cecilia did confirm to me: women need sex every bit as much as men and more.

* * *

The sheer abundance of sex with Cecilia isn't the only reason I no longer feel "unloved."

Food poisoning will put a horse off his feed. Cecilia lied, betrayed, stole, extorted, assaulted, ransacked and imprisoned. It could have been much worse. But, it does make one pause.

Life is good without having to please a woman. After Cecilia, it is *very good.*

It feels like getting out of prison.

A man who "needs" a woman is adding a boss at home to the one at work. My "unloved" feeling is why I put up with so much shit from Cecilia and other women over the years. *Never again!*

With the shift of power in society, a woman can be dangerous to a man. She might be PMS and put him in jail for defying her. At the drop of a hat, she can take his home and children, and then force him to support her for life.

In our world, true love is *elusive,* to say the least. As Gerry and I discovered, a woman can vow eternal love one day and the next day she's gone. Why live for that? (I know men can be just as unfaithful to women.)

Many women want a family. They just don't want a man. Loving a man means accepting his leadership, supporting and nurturing him. They can't seem to do this any more. They are looking for wives themselves. As producer Linda Obst said, echoing Gloria Steinem, "We've become the men we wanted to marry."

So, in a sexually dysfunctional society, I'll settle for pure unadulterated *freedom* instead. I practice the yoga of doing exactly what I please every moment of my life. Is it a coincidence that another term for enlightenment is "liberation?"

* * *

Do I feel stupid about what I did?

No and Yes.

No. I believe that without Gerry and zero tolerance, the marriage had a chance. I loved Cecilia, and for a while, she loved me. I still believe that honest, loving, faithful, traditional women abound in Asia. But I was too love starved and immature to patiently find the right one.

Yes. I should never have married Cecilia after it became obvious that she was anything but submissive. I should have guessed that the reason for her cockiness was Gerry. But men and women who, like me, suffer from the scourge of feeling "unloved" will behave self destructively to get that love. They will ignore the warning signs.

They will endure a great deal of horse shit. They will give away their power.

The essence of masculinity is power. Any time a man gives his power to a woman, he is writing his epitaph and that of the relationship. Women do not respect men who pander to them.

From the beginning, I should not have tolerated Cecilia's behavior: the unwillingness to talk; the episode on our "engagement" night; the episode over the fruit lady etc. etc. All of these were signs to move on. But I patiently persisted because of her beauty and the degree of my need.

I now believe in paying attention to first impressions and attacks of "irrational" anxiety. Also, I believe in actions not words, and I don't expect people to change.

I've heard that we draw to ourselves the experiences we need. Obviously I wasn't ready for marriage. Cecilia gave me what I needed to mature. She was a mistake I needed to make. I am no longer that person.

I don't blame Cecilia. Her stock-in-trade was "love"; she was good at it. She used this talent to advance herself. She acted her age, which is more than I can say. She didn't have the nerve to tell Gerry she was married. Better keep him as insurance. This way, a spoiled girl could postpone growing up.

All marriages are gambles. When he wins, a gambler is a genius; when he loses, he's a fool. I've done both and take them in stride.

Half of all marriages end in failure; these *aren't* mail-order brides. Many people marry in conventional ways; they *still* don't know who their mate is. They *still* get betrayed.

My dad had said, "meet ten Filipinas, make a short list, and then select the best."

A starving man will not compare menus at ten restaurants.

But, *thanks to you, Cecilia*, I've got my pilot's license. I can take my time.

Next week, I'm off to Mexico City to meet a smart young web site designer who still has the virtues of a traditional woman. I'll let you know how it goes.

Epilogue: What I Believe

IN DEFENSE OF HETEROSEXUALITY

In 1997, the Canadian birth rate fell to its *lowest point in history,* 1.6 children per woman. This figure, which represents the number of children a woman has in her lifetime, is a decline of 60% from 1960 when the rate was 3.9 children. The birth rate has declined 15% in the last five years alone.

The declining birth rate is mirrored by the falling rate of marriages and rising rate of divorce. The current marriage rate (5 per 1000 population) is lower now than in 1931 during the Great Depression. It is down 44% from 1970. The divorce rate is up 35% from 1970. (Canadian Social Trends, Statistics Canada, Spring 2000.)

In my opinion, these statistics reveal a rapid breakdown in male-female relations that is undermining society and causing untold personal misery. The reason is that millions of young men and women *are* confused about their sexual identity. The cause is feminism, which teaches the young that sex roles are merely the product of social conditioning and are oppressive by definition.

This influence was prevalent in 65 female students I taught in 1999-2000 at the University of Winnipeg. These mainly 18 and 19 year-old women saw divorce, not marriage, as the defining moment in a woman's life. They believed marital breakup was inevitable and assumed they would have to support themselves and their children alone.

For example, they applauded Stella Kowalski for leaving Stanley in the movie version of *A Streetcar Named Desire*. Until then, they saw Stella, a pregnant housewife, as a "doormat" despite the fact that she was obviously very happy and in love.

These attitudes reflect the feminist orientation prevalent in society, especially in government, the media and education. For more than three decades, feminists have been teaching young women to make career their first priority. They are teaching them to see men as violent predators, and to reject traditional sex roles and gender division altogether.

Every human being is entitled to fulfill her career aspirations. It would be absurd to ask contemporary women to view marriage as their only route to economic wellbeing. The question is one of priority. Which is more important? Becoming a wife and mother? Or developing a career and becoming "independent"? A woman has to make one her priority because these paths tend to conflict, both practically and philosophically.

A woman can always get a career. The optimum time to marry and start a family is in her twenties. Nature has made young women most attractive to men and most capable of bearing and raising children. The statistics show that, thanks to the influence of feminism, thousands of women (and by extension, men) are missing the boat, with dire consequences for both them and society.

* * *

In *The Flight from Woman (1964)*, Dr. Karl Stern, a distinguished psychiatrist, defined the difference between the masculine and the feminine.

Dr. Stern's ideas are a variation on the old adage, "The man makes the house, the woman makes the home." They are useful to understanding the feminist attack on traditional sex roles.

Dr. Stern says the essence of masculinity is *"power" or mastery over the physical environment.* Men are do'ers, fixers, adventurers, protectors and providers. Men are drawn to use reason and science to overcome the physical world.

The essence of femininity, Dr. Stern says, is *"love"— mastery over the spiritual environment.* Unlike men, women do not stand outside of creation and relate using abstract ideas. They are part of creation, in tune with people, emotion, intuition and what Dr. Stern calls "poetic knowledge."

Unlike men, women do not *do,* they *are.* They do not go out to the physical world; they go in to the moral realm. Their power is their beauty, wisdom, grace and love. These qualities fit them for their role as nurturer and "home" maker.

Of course, Stern is describing extremes. Most of us fall somewhere along the continuum. Nevertheless these distinctions are useful to understanding the fundamental difference between the sexes.

* * *

In the past, women made men feel powerful. Men then devoted their power to the service of women (and children). The male quest for mastery and money is pretty empty by itself. Women provided a higher purpose. Men made the living. Women made life *worth living.*

Women have been selected by nature for a task far more important than *anything* men do. She creates life. She creates family, the only *living thing* which succeeds us when we die, our only link to eternity. We can aspire to no higher achievement than a healthy loving family.

By putting her family first, a woman is the nucleus of a successful family. She starts the circuit of love, which inspires a man to take on the responsibilities of family. She creates the environment which restores the man and nourishes and shapes the next generation.

"Equality" makes sense only as a marriage of these two different *kinds* of power. To form durable unions, women should cede male-style power to men. A man will do his best for a woman who respects his masculinity. Men and women were meant to specialize in *different* areas of the psyche. In marriage, we were meant to find psychic *completion.*

Feminism has taught women to seek male-style power *for them-selves* and to compete for it with men. Dr. Stern describes them as "phallic women." But as they gain phallic power, such women are losing their own uniquely female power. How can they love someone with whom they compete?

Teaching women to seek male-style power is the same as injecting them with testosterone. Taking this power from men and giving it to women is emasculating men. In short, power = penis. In heterosexual relationships, only one is necessary. Sexual identity is undermined, if not dissolved when women invade the masculine realm, and when men are asked to fill the vacuum left by women.

But this is exactly what the radical feminists want. They seek to erase gender altogether by incorporating male and female power in one person. Thus women are encouraged to be more like men and vice versa.

Their androgynous vision of society is proving to be a recipe for sexual and social suicide. Opposite attracts; same repels. *Androgens don't need anyone else.* And they don't reproduce, except with a test tube.

* * *

The praiseworthy goal of equal economic and political status for women has largely been achieved. Today feminism has morphed into a potent and virulent disease attacking the biological and cultural foundations of society. It represents a raw hunger for power, a vicious hatred of men, and a shameful abdication and devaluation of the feminine.

Many radical feminist leaders are lesbians and believe lesbianism is the logical progression of feminism. Feminists and homosexuals hide behind an image of being a persecuted minority seeking only tolerance and equality. In fact, they wish to undermine heterosexuality. "Queer politics is no longer content to carve out a buffer zone for a minoritized and protected subculture," a gay manifesto *Fear of a*

Queer Planet declares. Its goal is "to challenge the pervasive hetero-normativity of modern societies."

Many feminists and homosexuals believe heterosexuality and the nuclear family are inherently evil. In the book, *Feminist Politics and Human Nature,* Alison Jagger writes that the nuclear family is "a cornerstone of woman's oppression: it enforces women's dependence on men, it enforces heterosexuality and it imposes the prevailing masculine and feminine character structures on the next generation."

Through their powerful influence in government, media and education, feminists are transforming society. Today, traditional sex roles are encouraged only if they are practiced by the *reverse* sex. Men who stay home with the kids are applauded. Women who are cops or mountain climbers are considered role models. But if the same roles are encouraged for the traditional sexes, suddenly they become "sexist". Men are taught to feel ashamed of their natural competitive nature or sexual drives. Women are stigmatized for wanting to be wives and mothers.

This kind of dogma is as dangerous as it is unnatural. Masculinity and femininity are hard wired into the brain of the fetus. (*See Anne Moir and David Jessel, Brain Sex: The Real Difference Between Men and Women,*1992). For example, testosterone levels in males are twenty times that of females. Culture elaborates and nuances these innate differences by way of sex roles. Male and female sex roles are essential to our development as individuals. To tell young people that male and female sexual identity has no basis in biology is dishonest. To discourage them from expressing their natural heterosexual inclinations is perverse.

The feminist attempt to erase gender strikes me as homosexual in character. How else can we explain the concerted attempt to alienate young women from men, and from the institution of marriage? How else can we explain the attempt to characterize heterosexual sex as rape? And what about the fanatical refusal to allow anything positive to be said about traditional heterosexual roles?

* * *

The main target of feminists is the white male who is accused of having always oppressed women as well as the poor and people of other races. Feminists believe all of western civilization is nothing but a rationalization for white male domination. The solution: eliminate culture and replace it with the experience of the "oppressed." Use "human rights" and "preferential hiring" to place the "oppressed" mainly women and certain minorities, in positions of power regardless of their qualifications. Thus our universities have become a joke and men are now discriminated against in education and in the workplace.

The oppression of women by men is a myth. In the past, women have been discouraged from assuming the male role. This is not the same as being oppressed. In fact, women have always been exempted from combat and were often protected from hard manual labor. Even today, men make up 95% of work place fatalities. Only feminists think the female role is oppressive. The almost two million U.S., Canadian and British men who died in two World Wars might have preferred it.

In general, feminists have taken power through an effective campaign of demonizing men. Women are seen as helpless victims from heaven; men are violent predators from hell. Women's Studies Departments at hundreds of universities, government programs, movies, TV and print all reinforce these stereotypes. The hysteria feminists are directing against men would not be tolerated against any other social group.

For example, men are said to be rapists. A much-quoted Ms. Magazine survey claimed that 25% of American women said they'd been raped by the time they reached college. It turns out, they defined "rape", as succumbing to a man's "continual arguments and pressure." This is typical of the inflation of the vocabulary of abuse.

In general, feminists extrapolate from a relatively small number of incidents to characterize *all men* as violent oppressors. Thus they have destroyed the trust which is the cornerstone of heterosexual relationships.

In the home, feminists have wrested power from men and given it to women by the widespread "zero tolerance" policy. A woman need only claim that a man has touched her, or uttered a threat, and he will be jailed for domestic assault without any proof. In fact, she can invent any charge she wants and she can do it months or even years later. Every year thousands of law-abiding men like myself are abused and then jailed simply for trying to maintain order and civility in our homes. Under these circumstances, men are no more likely to marry than are women.

* * *

My contract to teach at the University of Winnipeg was not renewed because a few students slandered me. Again, this is a textbook example of how feminists take power from men. They convict men of "sexual harassment" which they now define as anything that makes one female feel "unsafe or uncomfortable."

My real crime: offering intellectual respectability for traditional male and female sex roles illustrated by an analysis of DH Lawrence, *Lady Chatterley's Lover;* Henry James, *Wings of the Dove;* Henrik Ibsen, *Hedda Gabler* and Anton Chekhov, *The Sea Gull.*

The majority of my female students were happy to receive intellectual support for becoming a wife and mother. Some of them thanked me after class. But, in the university's eyes, they don't count.

* * *

Radical feminists claim capitalism is an example of oppressive patriarchy. Ironically, feminism would not have succeeded if it didn't fit the corporate agenda. Why pay a man enough to support a family when you can get his wife working for the same amount as well? Double the workforce, double productivity and keep a lid on wages.

Our corporate leaders have other reasons for encouraging feminism. One is to divide and conquer. Keep men and women at each other's throats and they won't question the direction of society. Who better to emasculate men than women? But it goes deeper than that. Keep us isolated and alone, sex starved and dysfunctional, and we will be better consumers.

Big business wants us to define our identity solely in terms of what we produce and consume. It doesn't want us to get meaning from family roles that have nothing to do with the economy. Thus, mothers rush back to work six weeks after giving birth, leaving strangers earning minimum wage to raise their baby.

The traditional family is the last place where the father and mother can create a little world dedicated to something other than consumption. With the decline of the nation state, the family represents the last resistance to the corporate vision of life.

Steward Ewen, in his classic study of the advertising industry *Captains of Consciousness (1976)* cites advertising trade journals which talk about increasing consumption by undermining the traditional family. This is done by undermining the authority of men by empowering women and youths.

Have you noticed how many ads make women look smart and men look ridiculous? How many ads encourage sex role reversal? How many ads show people gaining happiness from consumer products instead of healthy male-female relationships?

Take the AT&T ad for example. The career woman comes home to an empty apartment. The warm glow from her computer greets her lovingly in masculine tones and says: "let's order out for pizza." This woman is a success in corporate terms: she is a producer, a consumer and nothing else.

Or take the Herbal Essence shampoo ad. A woman is getting off by washing her hair in the service station bathroom. She sounds like she's having an orgasm. The hapless young male trying to fix her engine is portrayed as impotent when the radiator "prematurely" spills over. She clearly doesn't need *him*. She has the shampoo.

Politicians do the bidding of their corporate masters. In Canada the feminist movement is entirely funded by the government and would hardly exist otherwise. In 1980 the National Action Committee on the Status of Women which claims to represent 3 million women tried to raise some money from its membership. It raised $7,800. The same year, it received $4.1 million from the federal government. (On this, I highly recommend Martin Loney's *The Pursuit of Divison: Race Gender and Preferential Hiring in Canada, 1998.*) The President of NACSW was recently quoted as saying half her membership is lesbian. Thus .3% of the population claim to represent the women of Canada.

Women are victims of this unholy alliance between big business, big government and feminism. An NBC poll released June 22, 2000 states that only 14% of women work for personal satisfaction. The rest work for money. If they could, one third of American women said they would prefer to work just part-time. Nearly as many would stay home and care for their family. And even more would prefer volunteer work to a full-time career.

"I think women, more than any other group are beginning to feel betrayed by work," work historian Benjamin Hunnicut told ABC News June 7. "That what they seek at work, this identity, community, meaning, is not being found." Psychologist Mary Piper shares a similar point of view. "The world of work is organized in a way that makes it very difficult to both work and be a loving, committed member of a family at the same time. I don't think women as a group are much happier now."

Are we Spartans who must draft all our women in the battle for more wealth?

As a society, are we so poor and greedy that we cannot free more of them to enrich their husbands and children?

Women have been tricked into abdicating their role as nurturers and mediators of spiritual values. Everyone — men, women and children — are suffering grievously from the deficiency of feminine values in the world. These qualities include grace, beauty, sweetness, intuition, tenderness and love.

Professor Ruth Wisse of Harvard University sums it up: "By defining relations between men and women in terms of power and competition instead of reciprocity and cooperation, the [women's] movement tore apart the most basic and fragile contract in human society, the unit from which all other social institutions draw their strength."

At the beginning of the 21st Century, our major challenge is to restore the respect given to traditional sex roles, and to the traditional family.

c.2000 Henry Makow Ph.D.
Henry Makow's e-mail address is silas_green@go.com